Tommaso I

# Developing a healthy self

## Artemíology in action

ISBN 978-1548508142

# Contents

“The best way to predict the future
is to invent it.”

Alan Kay

# Introduction

*"There is nothing as practical as a good theory."*

*Kurt Lewin*

***How to use this handbook.***

Life is about choices and responsibilities. Reading this book is your choice and it will be entirely up to you whether you will practise what is suggested here.

One of the questions I am frequently asked is "Can I do it?" or "Will I be able to get through this?" My answer is: P = M + S.

P stands for the power to introduce changes in your life. Change is possible provided that you have a combination of M (motivation) and S (skills). How motivated are you? If you are motivated, then I'll show you how to take care of yourself.

This is a practical guide, which provides step-by-step advice. At the end of each section you will find an 'Activity Box'. These boxes consist of two different sets of recommended activities, which I would encourage you to carry out before moving on to the next section.

The first set of activities is called *PAL,* which stands for *Pondering A Little*, and offers food for thought exercises. The second set is called *BIT*, which stands for *Behaviour Improvement Training*, and provides a range of recommended practical actions.

So, you will be asked to spend some time with your *PAL* and to do your *BIT*, each step of the way.

Do not rush through this guide as you would with an interesting novel, which you cannot put down. Do not put pressure on yourself, even if you are really looking forward to the next step.

This is not a book to read: it is a guide to interact with. Give yourself the time to go through each step thoroughly before you move on to the next.

### *What is Artemíology?*

Artemíology – from the old Greek word *άρτεμία*, artemía (soundness, health) – is a psychological approach whose main aim is the development of a healthy self.

Artemíology embraces the key elements of a human being.

First, it deals with our three components:

- physical: our body and the sensations we get from it, such as hunger, headaches or pleasure;
- emotional: our feelings and the moods we allow ourselves in, such as sadness, despair or joy;
- rational: our thoughts and the states of mind we experience, such as worry or concern.

Next, it works through our three levels:

- intrapersonal: our deeply rooted system of opinions about us and the world;
- personal: our choices;
- interpersonal: the way we relate to others.

Then, it helps us understand the impact in the present of past memories and future worries.

Finally, it shows us how to use our behaviours as tools for preventing problems and managing relapses.

Artemíology is, in essence, an integration of humanistic counselling and CBT, that is, cognitive behavioural therapy. However, unlike the two models above, artemíology places a substantial emphasis on prevention.

The specific tools and consolidated advice provided in the fifteen steps which make up this handbook will support those of you who are currently going through a difficult phase, and will show you how to navigate out of it. But, most importantly, will also increase your emotional resilience and raise your awareness, thus helping all of you avoid psychological problems in the future.

# First Part

# Components

# Chapter 1
# Sensations

*"Through our senses the world appears.*
*Through our reactions we create delusions.*
*Without reactions the world becomes clear."*

*Buddha*

***Your body knows better***

Why are we starting from the body? Why don't we go straight to our emotional or rational components? *"Mens sana in corpore sano"* (healthy mind within a healthy body), as the Romans used to say.

If you eat junk food, smoke, consume alcoholic drinks, frequently have tea and coffee and rarely put together seven-eight hours of sleep a night, why are you so surprised if you don't perform as well as you would like to, or if you often find yourself in a terrible state of mind?

Do I want to take all the fun out of your life? To the contrary, one of the purposes of this guide is to show you how to have plenty of fun and make the most of your life.

Statistics tell us that our life expectancy is improving. Yes, sure! But are our western populations healthier just because we live longer?

I remember having read somewhere that when a journalist congratulated the Italian researcher Rita Levi Montalcini, when she was awarded the Nobel prize for medicine, by saying "your research will allow us to live longer", she replied "my dear friend, the point is not to add days to our life, but life to our days."

This is exactly my point too! I take care of my body not because I want to live forever, but because I would like to be happy and functional for as long as the ticket for my life's show lasts.

How do we go about it, then? The first step of this chapter will address two topics: glucose level and balanced eating. The second step will explore the connections between body and mind.

# First Step
# Learning how to take care of our body

## *Glucose level: why does it matter?*

If you don't maintain a stable level of glucose in your bloodstream you may experience any or a combination of the following symptoms: nervousness, shakiness, headaches, feeling miserable for no apparent reason, lack of concentration, and tiredness.

I once saw a client that came to me complaining of tension and nervousness. I could have been a psychoanalyst or psychodynamic therapist recommending three sessions a week for the next two-three years. I could have been a traditional psychotherapist offering a weekly slot for the next twelve months.

I could have been an orthodox cognitive behavioural therapist and invite him to participate in a 25-session programme of therapy. For his good luck, I am a psychologist who practises artemiology and I saw him just three times.

How was this possible? Am I a miracle worker? Of course I am not!

During the initial consultation, I simply asked him "what do you have for breakfast?" and when he replied that he had been skipping breakfast for the past three years and that the first food entering his body was a Danish pastry at around 10 am, I asked him to have a proper breakfast every day for the whole of the following week and gave him a few hints on how to go about it.

When he came for his second meeting, a week later, he was already feeling better and I used the second and third meetings to give him more information about the connections between his body and his mind, and that was it. I received an email from him a few weeks later where he confirmed his healthy condition and thanked me for having gone straight to the point.

To make sure that you keep your level of glucose stable all you are required to do is to have three regular meals a day (i.e. breakfast, lunch and supper), to increase the quality (note not the quantity) of complex carbohydrates (i.e. good bread, rice, potatoes) and to decrease the quantity of refined carbohydrates (i.e. sugar, cakes, biscuits) and junk food (i.e. crisps, confectionery, etc.). It is as simple as that!

Some say they don't have time for breakfast or lunch. That's a pretty lousy excuse. It takes twenty minutes to have a decent breakfast and you are better off trading twenty minutes in bed for the pleasure of a healthy start to your day: you will sleep better the coming nights if you have a more balanced approach to your daytime activities.

The same applies to lunch. Common excuses are "I am too busy to have a lunch break" or "my colleagues don't have one, it may look odd if I start having mine".

I am sure you can think of better things to do with your time and money than seeing a doctor or a therapist and that is where your unhealthy habits have brought you, or will bring you very soon.

You'd better make time for your lunch break, and, in time, you will gently and gradually appreciate how important your break is. You will notice that when you take your lunch break nothing terrible happens: the world still spins around, your school or your office building are still standing there and your study or work performance improves during the second part of the day.

After all, they don't pay you to keep your chair warm. They pay you for the quality of your work and your lunch break will improve that quality!

Nobody in the office is having a lunch break? Well, good luck to them! Would you like to keep on following them all the way down the cliff, like sheep after a blind shepherd?

Do they look like they are all doing fine? Ninety per cent of my clients tell me that they put on a brave face at work: they are not doing fine, at all. They just keep going and keep up with sad and unhealthy lifestyle choices.

A very successful professional once told me: "I feel like a rat on a treadmill. Always working. Never stopping. Earning a lot. Spending a lot. And at the end of it, what's left? I have been pushing too hard for too long and now here I am, feeling like a wretch."

***Balanced eating: missing information or misinformation?***

There are thousands of books out there dispensing information on new and old diets and not surprisingly so. The diet industry is a multi-billion pounds (or dollars) business.

Everybody seem to be a winner: book sellers and authors make huge profits, magazines and journalists take their share of the pie and people seem to find the answer to their prayer ‘want to look great without much effort’.

It stays a great business precisely because, in the long run, none of these diets work and people come back for more: if one of them worked, that would have been it! No more selling and buying, people would know what to do and how to go about it.

In other words, many people make a pretty good living out of exploiting others’ laziness and dumbness. Tired of being lazy and playing dumb? Well, here it goes, let’s do it!

Obesity is fast becoming a widespread problem in our western societies. However, in the vast majority of cases, it is not due to genetic factors or intervening diseases.

So, whether you would like to lose or gain weight it is a simple matter of input (what you allow into your body) and output (what you do with your body). Let's first clarify here some basic points about the input. The next step will show you how to put them into practice and will also deal with the output part of the equation.

How do you know when you are hungry? Do you eat when your stomach rumbles or when it's time to have a meal? Do you eat when you feel nervous or tired or when you are happy and relaxed?

Being aware of what kind of hunger you regularly experience is already a valuable step in the appropriate direction, because it allows you to respond to each stimulus with the proper behaviour.

If you are experiencing genuine hunger you'd better eat. If it is an emotional hunger, I will show you how to deal with it in the 'emotions' chapter of this guide. If you are hungry because you are worried about something, the 'thoughts' chapter will show you how to address it in a rational way.

If you would like to find out more about what to eat and when, you will find plenty of information in Appendix A (Frequently Asked Questions) and B (General Information).

Some people tell me “I know what to do, but I find it difficult to do it.” If this is you, you will see how the next steps will offer you advice as to ‘how’ to take good care of your body.

Activities Box 1.

Time for your *PAL …*
*Write down a list of things that you normally do and things that you do not normally do, when it comes to taking care of your body.*

and for your *BIT.*
*Begin putting the advice above into practice, starting from your daily breakfast and lunch break.*

## Second step
## Exploring the connections between body and mind

This step will show you the role played by three brain chemicals (serotonin, endorphin and BDNF) in your overall functioning and how to look after yourself by taking care of your body, while having a great time in the process.

***Serotonin.***

In pop psychology (i.e. articles in magazines, newspapers and self-help books) serotonin is usually depicted as the 'happy hormone'. Well, it isn't really like that. Serotonin is the brain chemical which helps you stabilise your mood and passes on the message "calm down, relax, and take it easy".

When you visit your GP and get prescribed Citalopram, Prozac, Seroxat or Lustral – that is a Selective Serotonin Reuptake Inhibitor, SSRI – what your little pill does for you is pretty straightforward: it allows you to re-use the serotonin that you are able to produce by inhibiting the functioning of your *cleaner* cells, thus having the same molecules of serotonin hitting your cell receptors repeatedly.

What many don't know is that you can increase your serotonin level by eating the appropriate food.

As you will see in a moment it is not difficult to do that and, at the same time, it is not difficult to prevent yourself from releasing enough serotonin either.

The little formula you want to keep in mind is S = C + T + VB6. To make sure that you are able to release serotonin when required, you want to eat C , that is, complex carbohydrates (i.e. bread, rice, pasta, etc.). T stands for tryptophan, which is an essential amino acid found in proteins.

Foods rich in tryptophan are: chicken, cheddar cheese, ground beef, tuna, tempeh, cottage cheese, tofu, salmon, scrambled eggs, spaghetti, kidney beans, quinoa, almonds, lentils, milk, soy milk and yogurt.

Vitamin B6 is found in almost everything we eat. Foods rich in B6 are: wheat germ, oats, baker's yeast, yeast extract, mackerel, liver, nuts, soya beans, potatoes, bananas, garden peas and green cabbage.

Now, you want to eat all three of the above during the day to do the trick, only two out of three won't do it. As you can see, eating lots of refined carbs and sugary stuff not only messes up your glucose level, but prevents you from releasing serotonin too!

Make sure that you don't overcook or fry your proteins. The more you cook them, the less nutrients you are getting from them. Naturally, I am not asking you to eat raw meat, but steaming, boiling, pressure cooking and grilling (exactly in this order) are much better than frying or microwaving.

When it comes to vitamin B6, many tell me "No problem there, I am having lots of supplements." Well, that could be precisely the problem, instead.

You see, eating too much of a particular vitamin may throw your vitamins' balance off, resulting, in the long run, in damage to your health. If you are not allergic to certain types of food, my advice is to avoid supplements and get your vitamins directly from their natural sources.

If you have a varied and balanced eating style, you will provide your body with all the vitamins it requires.

### *Endorphins.*

Now, these are what we might call 'the happy hormones'. Research has shown that endorphins make us feel good about ourselves and a number of studies have associated endorphins with raised confidence and self-esteem.

So how do we get them flowing through our system? There are, at least, five ways to help our bodies release endorphins and, not surprisingly, they are all connected to our senses. Let's introduce them, one by one.

1. Food.

   Yes! Here we go again. Your sense of taste can induce powerful pleasurable responses. So, how to go about it? The idea here is to make your eating pleasurable without having necessarily to favour sweet or very savoury foods.

In other words, you are encouraged to begin appreciating food for its natural taste, rather than over-spicing it. Make every eating moment a pleasurable one starting from your sight (i.e. put a nice table cloth down, choose cheerfully coloured plates). Then, have some flowers on your table and put your favourite music on.

Most importantly, eat slowly. You want to feel the taste of what you are eating. Fast eaters are more likely to become binge eaters, feel bloated or have digestive problems.

Apply the ancient Buddhist rule "Eat as you were drinking and drink as you were eating". That is, properly chew your food and swallow it when it's almost liquid and drink in sips.

I used to be a very fast eater myself and I have steadily and gradually changed this unhealthy habit by initially leaving my fork or spoon on the table each time I had used it to place food in my mouth.

I would pick it up again only when I had properly masticated and swallowed what I had in my mouth first. It felt a bit weird, at the beginning, but it worked! Now, I can hold cutlery in my hand *and* eat slowly, at the same time.

2. Exercise.

Exercising is a well-known way to induce the release of endorphins so much so that some can actually overdo it, like sufferers of anorexia who get the 'runners high'.

The healthy approach to exercising is to make sure it is easy and natural. Do it when, how and where you feel like doing it and do not push yourself too hard.

You are not competing for the next Olympic games and you are not a professional athlete. I have actually met clients that were even stricter in their exercise routine than professional athletes, by exercising too intensively and by not allowing their bodies enough weekly breaks. So, how much is enough?

You want to use your body **every day** for twenty minutes (two ten minute walks would do). Regularity is the key. There is not much point in killing yourself in the gym for two hours and then spending the rest of the week on your sofa in front of the TV.

Besides, exercising occasionally can actually seriously damage your health. Couch potatoes that once a week go crazy on a football pitch or a tennis court play Russian roulette with their hearts. Now you know. Don't risk a heart attack. If you feel like having fun with your friends for the occasional game, make sure your move your body every day to get ready for it.

Do I hear your usual excuse again? "I would love to, but I have no time." Set your alarm clock ten minutes earlier and walk around your house, or walk around your school or office block.

Do not do the 'stressful walk', that is, going from A to B at your highest speed, wearing high heels shoes and thinking of your exams, your bills, your mortgage, your car, your job and your love life, at the same time.

Do the ‘nice and easy walk’, that is, going from A to B by starting slowly and then gently increasing your pace and then gradually decreasing it, wearing comfortable shoes (you can always get changed once at school or in the office) and think of nothing, just enjoy feeling your body move.

I have become aware over the past few years of how gentle body movements can improve our overall wellbeing. As a result, in May 2005, I have created ‘Peaceflow’, a practice where simple psychological techniques are integrated with a number of gentle bodywork sequences. The regular practice of Peaceflow can provide a pleasurable alternative to more traditional forms of exercise. You can find out more about Peaceflow by visiting its dedicated website: www.peaceflow.org

3. Music.

Listening to your favourite kind of music does help you release endorphins too, so go for it. Make the most of your smartphone or mp3 player and enjoy your music!

4. Laughter.

There may be days when something really funny happens or one of your school mates or colleagues keeps on cracking one great joke after another. There may be days when not even a little smile crosses your face. Why is that?

Laughter is healthy, so make sure that you create a 'humour corner' at home. Your humour corner will have a sample of the things that make you laugh (i.e. books of quotes, jokes, prose, cartoons, DVDs or videos).

Make sure that when you are back at home from school or work that is the first place you visit. Pick something and have a laugh. This will also help you close mentally your working day and start your personal time.

5. Relaxation, meditation or prayer.

I have placed them together because, depending on your religious beliefs and lifestyle you are obviously free to decide which ones are for you. I will teach you some relaxation techniques, as part of the emotional management programme. If you are already into meditation or prayer, now you have one more reason to practise it.

***Brain-derived neurotropic factor (BDNF).***

BDNF is a brain chemical that, among other things, helps brain cells in the hippocampus regrow, thus counterbalancing the damage done by the stress hormone cortisol. To raise your BDNF levels you can:

1. Exercise.

2. Eat omega-3 oils, which you can find in oily fish (salmon, herring, mackerel, sardines), walnuts and olive oil.

3. Have acupuncture or practise Peaceflow, Yoga or Tai chi.

Activities Box 2.

Time for your *PAL …*
*Write down a list of the things that you already do to take care of your glucose, serotonin, endorphin and BDNF levels.*

and for your *BIT.*
*Begin putting the advice provided in this step into practice by making a plan of how you would like to introduce, nicely and gradually, the changes in your lifestyle which will allow you to release enough serotonin, endorphins and BDNF to keep you out of trouble.*

# Chapter 2
# Emotions

*"Learn the difference between responding and reacting."*

*Buddha*

## Third step
## Recognising your emotional states

***Getting ready.***

The first question I would like to ask you is "Where do you think emotions come from?"

You may say "from my mind" or "from the external environment". Naturally, we do know that, in the end, all incoming stimuli and information are processed by our brain. However, it may be helpful to note here that while at times we are aware of how some feelings come from an internal place (i.e. you wake up in the morning feeling happy or sad), other times they seem to come from external sources (i.e. the computer that crashes and drives us mad, the school mate or colleague making a stupid remark that triggers an angry response).

Identifying the perceived source of a given emotion can be very useful, because it can help us deal with it appropriately.

Generally speaking, most of us don't have a clue about how to deal with emotions. This is not because we are weak, stupid or faulty. This is simply because we are taught Geography, History and Maths and we are not taught how to tackle basic facts of life.

We learn about places 10,000 miles away from home and about events happened 2,000 years ago and we learn nothing about ourselves!

I love Geography and History, so don't get me wrong. However, I would have loved the opportunity to have had somebody coming in my class, at least once a month, to teach me how to take care of my body, how to deal with my emotions and how to address my rational concerns.

If you are going somewhere, it helps to know where you are going. You are more likely to get there, I suppose. So, what is the goal of learning emotional management?

Well, for a start, this is not about brainwashing or re-programming. Emotional management is about learning how to deal with emotions in such a way as to not upset ourselves and others more than it would be appropriate – depending on the specific life event you are experiencing.

Our goal is graphically illustrated in figure 1 below.

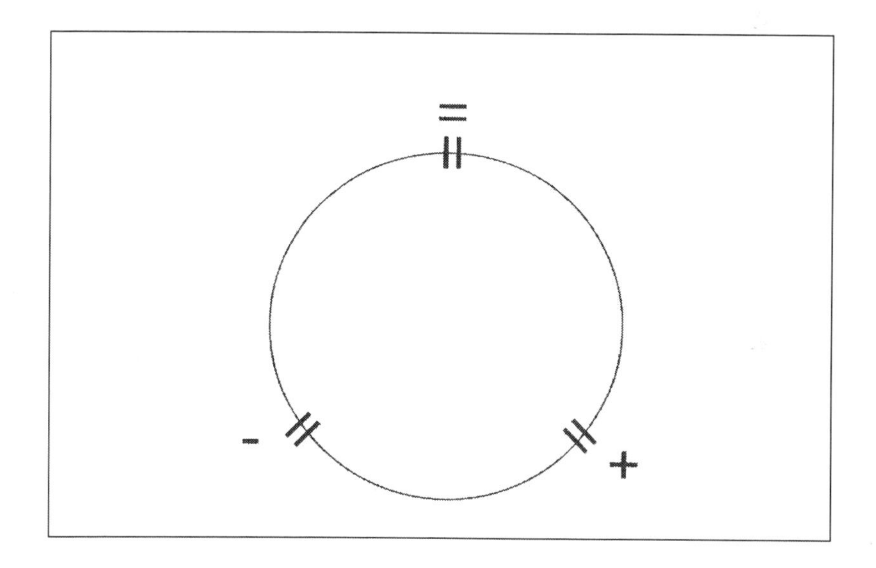


Figure 1. The Emotional Management Process

As you can see, our goal is to get you, first, from a mental place where you are experiencing negative feelings ( - ) to a place where you feel much more relaxed and calm ( = ). Then, I will show you how to move from the peaceful place to a happier one ( + ).

This is, by no means, the end of the story. This is just how we are going to progress through the emotional component. There is a healthier, more useful and helpful territory for you to be in and the ‘thoughts’ chapter of this guide will show you how to get there.

Some people ask me “why can’t we get directly from the negative place to the positive one?” as it looks like you are doubling the journey when you move first to the peaceful place.

Well, in real life sometimes shortcuts are not always as convenient as they may appear to be, at first sight.

As humans, we greatly benefit from getting first to a calmer place as a healthy way of processing negative feelings. Being at peace is a great place for you to be: happiness is like a flash of lightning, it comes, gets you high and then returns to the universe.

Peace, instead, is a place which you can inhabit.

Furthermore, when you are feeling really low, what do you think your response will be if somebody were to remind you of times when you were very happy?

You are most likely to feel even more the gap between where you are now and where you have been – or you could be now or in the future, if you weren't feeling that miserable – and this will hurt even more.

The recommendation of going about your person care 'nicely and gently' does not apply only to your daily exercise routine: it is valuable advice worth applying to how we deal with our emotions too.

***How have you been dealing with your emotions so far.***

There are three different ways in which we can respond to emotions. We can call these ways 'modalities' to help remind ourselves that we do have a choice as to which one we decide to apply to our everyday life circumstances.

First Modality: Action-Reaction Mode.

Sometime we respond to emotions by reacting to them. We can do so in three different ways: we may lash out, take in or displace.

***Lashing out.***

When we lash out at somebody who has been abusive or whom we view as the cause of our current emotional distress, we are simply trying to throw the negative emotional energy back to where it comes from.

So, although we may hit back for many different reasons, when we lash out our response is direct and explicit: direct, because there is no time-gap between the emotions impacting on us (action) and our reaction; explicit, because we openly and clearly display our emotional state.

Pop psychology publications may suggest lashing out in a controlled way (i.e. punching a pillow) as a way of releasing tension or anger. Such recommendations are pure nonsense!

When we punch a pillow we are teaching ourselves that it is ok to punch and, in so doing, we are consolidating the use of a violent and unhealthy behaviour. Today we punch a pillow, tomorrow we may punch a person.

***Taking in.***

We may also respond to emotions in a direct and implicit way. We minimise the importance of what is happening to us, or try to ignore it altogether.

We don't show our feelings and, most of the times, don't even share our emotional states with somebody close to us. We 'bottle things up', as they say in British English.

But emotions do not vanish just because we have decided to ignore them. So, where do they go? We are simply sweeping them under the carpet, or to use another metaphor, we are letting them sink deep down in our emotional container, day after day, week after week, month after month. Then one day we wake up, we feel miserable and depressed. We feel that 'we have had enough' and we don't know what's going on.

We have allowed these small time-bombs to sink in and now they are going off. We have lost track of hundreds of 'non important' feelings we failed to acknowledge at the appropriate time and now they have become a big scary ghost who has come back to haunt us.

***Displacing.***

We may also redirect (displace) the emotions onto somebody or something else rather than addressing them directly.

This happens when, for example, negative emotions originate at school or in the work environment and we displace them onto a family member at home or vice versa, or when we displace our boredom or sadness by eating or drinking compulsively or by starving ourselves.

When we displace, on the one hand, we don't deal with the original negative emotion and, hence, we maintain the source of personal distress, while, on the other, we create new negative emotions by placing unnecessary pressure on ourselves or others.

Second Modality: Action-Proaction Mode.

'Proactive' is an American word initially used in business, which has then leaked into common spoken English. While trying to be one step ahead of the competition may serve a commercial purpose in the workplace, it does not make much sense when it comes to dealing with our emotions. We can be proactive in two ways: by keeping on interrupting our interlocutor, or by daydreaming.

***Interrupting.***

Every time two humans interact there are at least three channels exchanging information, which gets activated. We sense the other's presence with our body, we get in touch with their feelings, we rationally engage with them.

When we keep on interrupting our interlocutor our body is still there, but we respond emotionally and rationally *before* the other has had the chance to complete what they are saying (action) and, hence, our response starts *before* we can receive a full account of what the other really means to say or do.

Now, how can we appropriately deal with emotions if we are not fully aware of what is happening to us? When we interrupt our interlocutor we are only making ourselves emotionally vulnerable.

The 'other' may have a communication style whereby they normally start with the good news (i.e. paying you a compliment, or saying something positive about your contribution to a project) and then they bring in the bad news (i.e. saying what they don't like about you, or criticising some of your professional choices).

If you interrupt and start your emotional response after the good news you are exposing yourself to the full impact of the bad news.

Others have a communication style whereby they usually start with the bad news and then they introduce the good news. If you interrupt and start your emotional response after the initial criticism you will find it very difficult to accept the good news – if you ever get to hear them, that is!

### *Daydreaming.*

We all switch off from reality and switch on daydreaming mode for a while during the day. There is nothing unhealthy about it.

However, some people spend long periods of time in 'daydreaming mode' and some use it as a regular way of dealing with emotions. When the latter applies we allow our response to start – that is, switching off our mind and landing in a parallel dimension – *before* we can be fully aware of what is happening around us. The real life event is still going on and we decide to leave and go somewhere else.

The more time we spend in our fantasyland and the more energy we put into making it a wonderful place to be, the less time and energy we have to make our real life a more exciting, stimulating and rewarding place to be.

Over time our fantasyland becomes a black hole which sucks in the best of us and leaves behind an everyday life ever more ordinary, dull and miserable.

As I have just said, a little bit of daydreaming can be useful and I will show you in due course how to make the most of it, when you feel like switching off. However, some people escape life and hide in their parallel dimension as a way of dealing with negative feelings and this is neither healthy, nor helpful.

***How to deal with your feelings in a healthy, useful and helpful way.***

When we experience negative feelings the 'smoke detectors' in our emotional brain (the amygdalae) go off. Now, if we were to deal with a real smoke detector going off at home because we left a pan of boiling water in the kitchen, we would follow the steps below:

- ✓ switch off the hob
- ✓ throw away the water
- ✓ open the window to let the smoke out
- ✓ manually disconnect the smoke detector
- ✓ make sure that there's no smoke left in the room
- ✓ reset the fire alarm system
- ✓ manually re-connect the smoke detector

When we are dealing with emotional distress, instead, what do we do? As we have just seen, we may:

- scream at somebody or hit something as we convulsively deal with the pan (lashing out)
- pretend nothing is happening (taking in)
- go down to the pub for a few drinks (displacing)
- close our eyes and think about our next holiday (daydreaming).

We have seen so far how *not to* respond to negative emotions. The following section and the next three steps will show you how to deal with them.

## Third Modality: Action~Pre-action Mode.

First of all, what does 'pre-action' mean? The 'pre' stands for 'preventative' and for 'preliminary'.

*Preventative,* because if you decide to follow my advice you will not get into trouble by lashing out, taking in, displacing, interrupting or daydreaming. There is only one of you and if you direct yourself in one direction, you will not be able to get somewhere else, at the same time. Imagine you are in a big room and there are six doors in front of you.

If you open and go through one of them, you won't be able to enter any of the remaining five doors simultaneously. It is very important to wait and give ourselves the opportunity to choose the proper *way in* our emotional self.

*Preliminary,* because when you go through the appropriate door, you will find yourself in a nice reception room furnished with a comfortable sofa and a big wardrobe.

You will want to give yourself the time to decide which room to go next (i.e. kitchen, living room, bathroom or bedroom) and to choose which garment to pick from the wardrobe accordingly.

Most of the time there is absolutely nothing wrong with us: we are simply not wearing appropriately for the occasion.

You will not feel comfortable jogging in the park in high heels, even if the weather is gorgeous! There is nothing wrong with you or with the park, it is just that you are not wearing the right gear.

So how do we get into pre-active mode? First, we want to get hold of some little tools: a small week-at-a-glance diary, a few post-it notes to stick to the inside back cover of the diary and a pen or a pencil, or you can use the 'notes' facility of your smartphone.

Make sure that you have the above with you at all times over the next few weeks. It is not difficult: ladies carry their bags with them all the time and guys have pockets or briefcases.

Then, follow the steps below:

1. When you feel the negative emotion, write down briefly 'what' is going on, 'how' you feel about it (i.e. have received a phone call from my ex-partner – feel very sad we are no longer together), and give a number to the note.

2. Then, make an appointment with yourself to deal with it. You ask yourself two questions: *when* is the appropriate time and *where* is the suitable place to deal with it? For now a ten-minute appointment would do.

3. The answer to the above question will never be ‘here and now’. Whatever feelings you are dealing with, you are not a brain surgeon and nobody will die if you give yourself at least a ten-minute gap before addressing the negative emotion.

4. Jot down the appointment in the diary (i.e. today at 2 pm deal with note n. 3) and make sure that you remind yourself of the appointment (i.e. by setting an alarm clock on your smartphone, or by sticking a note on your PC monitor).

5. When the time comes and you are in a proper place, for the time being just close your eyes, close your mouth, take a few deep breaths, read through your note and see how you feel.

In the next steps of this guide I will show you a number of techniques that you can practise at the time that you have scheduled. For now, it is important that you begin with practising first the art of making time for yourself, and this is what the pre-active mode is about.

I can teach you a number of useful techniques but if you don't start making time for yourself, you won't be able to practise any of them.

Emotions can come our way according to two variables, which are independent of one another: intensity and urgency.

So a feeling can be very intense (i.e. deep sadness, strong anger) and, at the same time, we may not feel a particular urgency to deal with it, or, on the other hand, it can be quite trivial (i.e. a bit of boredom), and we may feel that the sooner we get it out of the way, the better.

Practising getting yourself into pre-active mode will improve your ability of recognising your emotional states and of creating time to deal with them accordingly.

How does getting into pre-active mode work in practice? I will offer you now a real life example.

Some time ago a lady came to me to receive help in dealing with an anger management problem. She was not getting along with her new boss and, at the same time, she liked her job and had a big mortgage to pay. So, leaving her job was not an option but her new manager was driving her mad and she was afraid that sooner, rather than later, she would have punched the guy in his face (incidentally, she was a 6’2” tall woman).

When I introduced the different modalities and I suggested her to get into the pre-active mode during the next few days, I could see how puzzled she was by the fact that it seemed like she had nothing to do to help herself over the next week.

However, when she came back for the following meeting, she had an interesting story to tell. It was the story of what had happened one day during that week.

One morning she felt like the pressure started building up at work and decided to go for a quick break. She walked down a few blocks and popped into a shop.

As she collects Swatch watches, she felt like treating herself to a new one. She was walking back to the office when she realised that she had left the watch she was wearing by the till, so she made her way back to the shop and, to try to calm herself down she kept on saying things like “everything is going to be ok, don’t worry”, “there was nobody in the shop so the assistant has surely noticed your watch by the till and he is keeping it in a safe place for you”.

However, when she got there the assistant said he did not notice anything and the watch was not there anymore! She said to me: “Tommaso, my first thought was: this cheat! He has got it and now he’s pretending he knows nothing about it! I could see myself grabbing his tie and punching him with all my strength. But, at the same time, I visualised your face and you were telling me ‘Please, don’t do this, get into pre-active mode’. So, I gave the guy my business card and shouted at him ‘Here, this is my number, if you do find my watch call me’ and stormed out of the shop. I walked into a café, got out my diary, filled in a post-it note, made an appointment with myself (that night at home looked like a proper time and place) and returned to the office.”

She told me that, although she did not know what to do with her negative feelings once back home, she followed my advice of closing her eyes, closing her mouth and taking a few deep breaths. She then read what she had written on her post-it that morning and actually had a laugh, as 90% of the words she used were swear words. She took comfort in toying with her collection of watches for a while and, eventually, sent an email to the company asking if they could send her the same watch she had lost.

What's so special about the above story? Well, for a start the simple fact that, because of what had happened in the shop, that could have been the day she could have displaced her anger towards her boss: she didn't.

She told me that writing down her feelings, almost immediately, really helped and it also helped knowing that she had made time to deal with it. She managed to have a decent remaining part of the day at work and eventually was able to deal with it, even without knowing precisely how to go about it.

So, why is getting into pre-active mode a first step in the appropriate direction? Writing down very briefly what is going on and how we feel about it is helpful because we begin an opening process whereby we allow negative feelings out of our system. Writing is also useful because it is empowering to know that we can identify and name what is happening and this helps the feeling that we can do something about it.

A young lady suffering from bulimia, once told me how good she felt about knowing that there was so much that she could do to help herself and to leave behind her past self-defeating attitude towards her emotional issues.

Creating time just for you, as you do when you make an appointment and you book it in your diary, is one of the most precious gifts you can give to yourself: there is nothing more valuable than your health and your time.

Some of you may find it difficult to grant yourself permission to take care of your own issues. Sensitive and nice people are brought up to think that others always come first. I am not suggesting here that you would better mind your own business and disregard anybody else's problems. I am saying that we can, at the same time, take good care of ourselves **and** of others.

Think about it for a moment. How can you really be able to be there for others and guarantee an acceptable degree of continuity and quality in the care you offer, if you don't take good care of your own issues?

Do you remember what the cabin crew say when we are on a plane and about to take off? In an emergency, first adjust the oxygen mask on yourself and then help others. We can carry on being nice, friendly and supportive as much as we want and, at the same time, we can set aside a few moments during the day to deal with our issues and recharge our batteries.

Activities Box 3.

Time for your *PAL* …
*How have you dealt with your emotions so far? Have you been mostly lashing out, taking in, displacing, interrupting or daydreaming?*

and for your *BIT.*
*Get yourself the tools required to practise the pre-active mode and go for it!*

# Emotions

## Fourth Step
## Listening to your emotional self

Now that you know how to get ready for the journey through your emotional land, thanks to the practice of getting into pre-active mode, let's see how you can move from a situation where you experience negative feelings to one where you feel happy.

The first step is to change from feeling negative emotions to being at peace with yourself and with the world.

Some people find it very difficult to let themselves go with the flow and relax, even for very short periods of time. Their rational mind is constantly switched on as they try to control every behaviour and scrutinise each sensation.

This inability to de-stress affects many well-educated professionals who make a very sophisticated use of their minds.

However, they may push a bit too far and send their brains into over-drive: in such cases the fatigued and over-spinning rational mind completely takes over from the emotional one and the person gets stuck in a vicious spiral of negative automatic thoughts.

Some get to a point where they lack the energy to go – as a result of wasting a vast amount of resources on unnecessary activities – and break down. Others find it difficult to stay still, even for just five consecutive seconds.

When I ask my clients for a list of relaxing activities, they usually come up with activities which provide distraction rather than relaxation, such as watching the television, playing a game, going to the movies, etc.

Distracting our rational mind is naturally healthy and useful and we will talk about this later when we will introduce the steps associated with the rational component of this personal development journey. However, here we are interested in those activities that provide a connection with our emotional self.

Given that the connections between our emotional brain and our body are much denser than the ones between the emotional and rational areas of our brain, it makes sense to start by showing you, first, how to relax your body and then how to relax your mind. To do that I will teach you now two simple techniques: the Basic Body Relaxation and the Insight Breathing.

***Basic Body Relaxation (BBR).***

Sit comfortably somewhere, loose any tight clothing (i.e. belts, ties, bras, etc.), close your eyes and mouth and begin slowing down the pace of your breathing. Your first goal is to make sure that your breathing is slow and deep.

If you breathe in and out through your nose, you will be able to check the pace of your breathing: a fast pace will be easily heard, due to the noise generated as the flow of air rushes through your nostrils, while a slow one will be totally unheard.

To make sure that your breathing is deep, that is, that you are making a full use of your respiratory system rather than just of the upper part of your chest (as we normally do), you may wish to place one of your hands on your abdomen.

Place it gently, without applying any pressure, and you will be able to feel your hand going up and down as you breathe deeply in and out.

This will give you an awareness of how deep you are breathing and, at the same time, will result in a pleasant and soothing sensation. When your breathing is slow and deep you are also, by default, providing your body with a good supply of oxygen.

After about three minutes of the above you may now start focusing on your body. Remember that at this point you are still with your eyes and mouth closed and you are breathing slowly and deeply.

Focus first on your feet. Feel them more and more relaxed as you keep on breathing in and out. Feel them increasingly heavier as you are experiencing this pleasant sensation of relaxation.

Now, move this sensation of heaviness and relaxation gently and gradually up to your calves and do exactly the same: first feel them more and more relaxed, as you keep on breathing in and out and then feel them heavier. Move gently up to each part of your body until you will have reached and totally relaxed your head.

It normally takes five minutes to carry out this exercise, so it is possible to slot it in anywhere you are (i.e. home, office, restaurant, etc.).

Some of my clients practise the BBR in the toilets of their homes or offices, when there is no other quiet place available. I would encourage you to practice the BBR three times a day: in the morning, at some point in the middle of the day and in the evening.

This, naturally, in addition to the times when you would practice it as a way to get you from a negative emotional place to a positive one.

The practice of the BBR exercise has also two additional bonuses. The first is what we may call its 'expansion effect', that is, as your ability to relax improves and your experience of the exercise develops over time, you will see that you will feel relaxed for increasingly longer periods of times after your practice (i.e. you may start from feeling calm for the next 5-10 minutes and end up feeling relaxed for the next 2-3 hours).

When you are there with your eyes closed, your perception of the passing time also changes. They say that how long a minute feels depends on what side of the bathroom door you are on. In this case, it may feel like you have been there breathing in and out for ages and then when you open up your eyes you realise that only a few minutes have gone by.

The second is the anti-ageing effect that proper breathing has on our body in general and our skin in particular. Those who practise regularly any exercise associated with slow and deep breathing know what I am talking about and if you have ever met somebody who has been practising yoga or tai chi for a long period of time you will know what I mean too.

So, off you go. Don't just take my word for it. Practise the BBR and you will see for yourself.

### *Insight Breathing (IB).*

Now that you know how to relax your body, it is time to learn how to relax your mind. The most relaxing activity we can engage in is to focus our thoughts on our breathing. We can change our mood from sad to happy in a matter of minutes, but we can only be either relaxed or distressed at any one time. Therefore, when we focus our thoughts on the very basic fact that we are breathing, we cannot, at the same time, have our mind connected with other issues.

To do that, you start by practising the BBR and when you feel your body relaxed, then, move on and ask yourself three questions.

The first question is "What would you find most relaxing to imagine that you are breathing in and out of your body?" You may say "What kind of question is this? I am breathing air, what else would I breathe?" You see, we do know that we are breathing air, but the point here is what would you find 'most relaxing' to imagine that you are breathing.

When you are there with your eyes closed, seated comfortably, with your body relaxed and you ask yourself the above question, you never know what answer may come up.

Somebody once told me that he imagined himself seated at the bottom of a swimming pool, on one of these comfortable deck chairs, and he found it very relaxing to visualise himself breathing the 'blue' water of the pool. A lady found extremely calming the idea of breathing a bright orange 'plasmatic' substance made of some sort of 'fluid powder'.

Whatever comes up, it is absolutely fine. This is your exercise and you want to make sure that you visualise something that really relaxes you and if this is simply air, that's perfectly ok, as long as you ask the question.

The second question is "What colour(s) would you associate with calm, peace and relaxation?" There surely are colours you would associate with excitement, fear or sadness. Which one(s) would you link with relaxation?

If, for example, your chosen breathing medium is air and your relaxing colour is pale blue, then imagine that all the air around you is pale blue and that you are breathing in and out of your body pale blue air.

The third question is "What temperature would you associate with relaxation?"

Some like it hot or warm, others prefer it cold or cool. If you are not sure, you may try practising both and see which one makes you feel more relaxed. The main thing is that, as a result of asking yourself three questions about what you are breathing, you are totally focussed on just one thing: your breathing.

Therefore, you are effectively switching off your mind from the usual everyday worries and once you are there, silent, quiet, completely relaxed, physically and mentally disconnected from rational concerns, you will be able to listen to your emotional self. It is very difficult (if not impossible) to hear a single voice speaking to us if we keep on spinning around and are in a noisy and crowded open space. But, when we create a little time for ourselves and find a conveniently quiet place, we can hear clearly the sounds and words stemming directly from our emotional self.

I have been practising the BBR and the IB for many years now and I would like to offer you the following tip: even when you get to the point of mastering perfectly well the sequence of physical and mental steps, do take your time to move, nicely and gently, from one step to the other.

So, for example, with practice you may be tempted to start the IB straightaway from the final step, that is imagining that you are breathing warm, pale, blue air. However, I have found it much more helpful to keep moving gradually in that direction, by visualising first what is it that I am breathing, and moving then onto its colour and, finally, its temperature.

The same applies to the BBR. I still find it useful to first focus on slowing down the pace of my breathing, and then to concentrate on how deep it is, rather than trying to manage both at the same time. I would encourage you to practise the IB soon after the BBR. It may take between three and five minutes to carry out the IB, which added to the five minutes of the BBR makes a total time of eight to ten minutes.

Activities Box 4.

Time for your PAL …
How have you been trying to relax so far? Have you ever tried any of the above exercises or were you mostly distracting yourself?
Relaxing always involved an activity except for meditation

and for your BIT.
Practise the BBR and the IB three times a day.

## Fifth Step
## Talking to your emotional self

To make sure that you leave behind your negative feelings and consolidate your peaceful state of mind, I recommend the practice of a third exercise, which I have called the 3Bs.

**The 3 Breaths.**

The 3Bs consists of a series of nine breaths taken soon after we end the IB exercise. It is called the 3Bs because, as you will see in a moment, there is a minor variation in what we say to ourselves during the first, second and third of three, slow and deep, 'in and out' series of breaths.

Let's first see how you practise this technique and, then, I will tell you what is going on in your emotional self when you carry out this simple exercise.

Once you will have completed the IB, you will still be there seated comfortably with your eyes and mouth closed. Now, you say something to yourself in your mind, and at the same slow pace as you are breathing in and out.

Every time you breathe in, you say “I am here”. When you breathe out, the first series of three breaths you say “relaxed”, the second series you say “calm”, the third series you say “at peace”.

In addition, during the third series, when you say “at peace”, you also put a little smile on your face. The little smile fades away when you breathe in and say, in your mind, “I am here” and appears again on your face when you say, in your mind, “at peace”.

As you can see, it is a very simple exercise. So simple that it may make you wonder “do we need a psychologist to come and tell us to talk to ourselves like this?” Well, we have lost so much basic wisdom, over the past 50 years, as individuals and as a society, that nowadays I don’t take anything for granted when I deal with fellow human beings.

Having said that, there is a reason why I ask you to say to yourself exactly these words and precisely some words when you breathe in and others when you breathe out.

Using as a reference figure 2 may help follow my explanation.

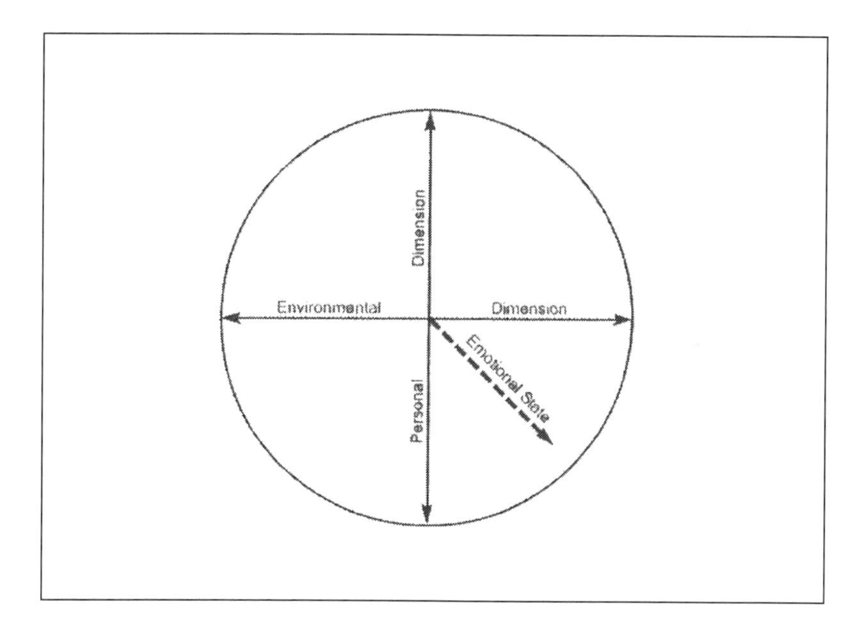


Figure. 2 The Three-Dimensional Being

The circle in figure 2 represents us as human beings. In reality each of us is a full, solid body, with its three dimensions (i.e. height, width and depth). The vertical axis is our 'Personal Dimension'. It represents where we are at a given time. So, for example, when we are connected with our past, we are centred somewhere along the lower segment of this vertical dimension, while when we are associated with our wishes and desires, that is with our future, we are somewhere along the upper segment. Depending on your personal approach to life, you may see the lower segment as the metaphor for the past, the unconscious, the deeper or inner self, the soul, etc.

Likewise, you may see the upper segment as representing the future, the conscious, the higher self, etc. This vertical 'Personal Dimension' (height) is our 'I am' co-ordinate.

The horizontal axis is our 'Environmental Dimension'. It represents how we relate with the world around us. So, for example, when we are emotionally connected with the things around us, with the physical environment, we are centred somewhere along the left segment, while when we are more associated with the persons around us, with the social environment, we are somewhere along the right segment. This horizontal dimension (width) is our 'here' co-ordinate.

Finally, the third dimension, the one that represents the depth co-ordinate of our being, is the one identified with our emotional state.

The first 'I' dimension answers the question "Who?", the second 'am' dimension answers the question "What?", the third 'here' dimension answers the question "How?" We may be sad, distressed and bored or we may be relaxed, calm and happy.

So, where might we be, at a given time, within our own planet? How do we know if we are centred or we are keeping ourselves at the edges of our world?

When we experience personal problems we keep ourselves on the edge of our planet and we face outwards turning our back on all the resources, which could help us feel differently about our situation (i.e. personal resources, like the awareness of where we have been or where we could be; or physical resources, like what we have acquired and achieved over the years; or social resources, like our friends and family).

What can we do about it, then? Well, we want to make sure that we face inwards rather than outwards and that we direct ourselves towards the centre of our planet, that is, towards a safer place.

How do we do that? We will see later how this will be achieved rationally, but now let's see how practising the 3Bs can help centre ourselves emotionally.

The 3Bs exercise asks you to say in your mind nine times "I am here" as you breathe in. When you breathe in, the movement is from the external environment towards you. Most importantly, there is only one place where the "I am" meets the "here" and this place is the centre of our being. Therefore, every time we slowly and deeply breathe in, we are moving towards our central, safer, place.

At the same time, we are also breathing out that we are relaxed, calm and at peace. This gives the third co-ordinate to our position within our being, ensuring that we don't move back to the periphery of our planet and we stay centred.

This time, as we breathe out, the movement is from our inner self towards the external environment. This and the fact that we put a little smile on our face, serves like a training activity to make sure that when the exercise is over, we can go back to our every day life *really* feeling relaxed, calmer and at peace.

I hope the above makes sense to you, but, even if it doesn't, don't worry.

Emotional techniques are not supposed to make sense rationally (it would be a disaster if the rational techniques would not make sense logically!) they are meant to nurture your emotional self.

The practise of the 3Bs does not take more than a couple of minutes, which added to the eight to ten minutes of the BBR + IB exercises gives a total of ten to twelve minutes.

As you can see, I am not asking you to leave your jobs, shave your heads, wear orange robes and sandals and start singing "Hare Krishna, hare, hare…" down the street. I am also not asking you to practise lengthy and complicated exercises, which would occupy considerable parts of your day.

If you are motivated to take care of yourself and look after your emotional wellbeing, a ten-minute practice, two or three times a day, is something that can easily be fitted into even the busiest daily schedules.

Activities Box 5.

Time for your *PAL* …
*Write down your thoughts about how differently you may deal with a given situation or event, when you are stressed and angry or when you are calm and relaxed.*

and for your *BIT.*
*Practise the 3Bs regularly (ideally three times a day, soon after the BBR and the IB).*

# Emotions

## Sixth Step
## Dealing with negative feelings

Now that you know how to take yourself from a place where you experience negative feelings to another where you feel calm and relaxed, let's see how to help you connect with strong positive emotions.

Before we do that, however, I would like to remind you that getting to a happy emotional state does not represent the end of your personal development journey, rather it is just a step forward in the appropriate direction.

When you disconnect from negative emotions to make peace with yourself and connect with positive ones, you are unplugging and re-plugging your emotional system, thus resetting your emotional self.

Now, let's get started with the final step of the emotional component.

***The Positive Association (PA).***

This technique has two main goals: to make sure that you strongly connect with a happy feeling and to remain associated with that positive emotion for a while.

To use a simple metaphor: imagine that you are on holiday. You are seated on a boat and you are exploring the coastline and the surrounding sea. The sea is crystal clear and, though you know that it is 60 or 70 meters deep, it looks like it is just 10 meters deep.

You notice something glistening at the bottom of the sea: it is a beautiful pearl. Your goal is to dive down there, catch the pearl and bring it back to the surface with you. Naturally, it would be appropriate to go down and, most importantly, to come up gently and gradually. Divers know that you are required to have a few compensation breaks on your way back to the surface to help the body re-adjust to the different pressures.

How do you practise the PA? First of all, you begin by practising the BBR, the IB and the 3Bs. When you feel you are in a much calmer place, then you stay there with your eyes closed and start the PA.

The Positive Association exercise consists of a number of steps. You go through these steps as you ‘dive down’ and you take the same steps backwards, when you return. One thing I am telling you now, so that I won’t repeat myself later, is that in between each step you are required to have your ‘decompression times’ in the form of breathing breaks.

To ensure that you go down and come back gradually, you take a few slow and deep breaths in between each step, to allow you the opportunity to fully connect with that particular step and to make sure that you move from one step to the next gently and gradually. How many you take is up to you. That depends on the time at your disposal.

If you were to take five deep breaths in between each step, the whole exercise would last approximately 15 minutes. If you have more time to enjoy this pleasurable exercise, you may take longer breaks.

Now, let’s introduce the steps.

1. Think of a very happy memory, or a very happy fantasy.

2. Identify the happiest part/scene of the above memory or fantasy.

3. Visualise on your inner screen the happiest part/scene. It doesn't matter if your visualisation is in black and white, colour or 3D, as long as the picture is clear, vivid and detailed.

4. Imagine you are in a cinema and you are seeing a movie. First, the picture you have just visualised becomes as big as a movie screen (quantitative change), and then, it starts getting in motion, like you were watching a real movie (qualitative change). You are starring in this movie and you can see yourself living this fantasy or re-living this very happy moment.

5. Step in the movie. Now you are not able to ***see*** yourself living or re-living the moment, you ***are*** living or re-living it. So, for example, let's assume that your fantasy is to lay down on a golden sandy beach, with the sun shining and a

turquoise sea only a few feet away. In the previous step – the cinema situation – you could see yourself lying down and enjoying the holiday, while in this step you can actually feel the sun on your skin and smell the sea breeze.

6. At this moment in time, you will feel very happy. Now, that you have found your 'pearl', it is time to grab it with both hands. So, ask yourself "Which part of my body feels happiest now?" or "Where is the centre of my happiness?" You don't want to analyse yourself now, this is meant to be a very straightforward question, which attracts a simple and intuitive answer. Some people say "the centre of my forehead", other "my neck" or "my tummy" or "my hands". There aren't right or wrong answers: just say in your mind what comes up first.

7. Spread this pleasant sensation of happiness all over your body now, nicely and gently. Make sure that you don't leave any part of your body out. So, for example, if your centre was your abdomen, start by spreading the pleasurable sensation of happiness all the

way down to your feet and then move up, right up to the top of your head or vice versa, as you like. How do you spread your sensation of happiness throughout your body? Some people associate happiness with a gentle touch and they imagine that a feather, a leaf or a small hand is touching them.

Others imagine an energy field or a liquid expanding all over their body. In one case the energy field was white and the liquid was orange. You may wish to try any of the above or find something different.

Once the pleasurable sensation of happiness has been spread all over your body, it is time to go back. However, as you move backwards you don't want to lose what you have achieved, you want to bring your 'pearl' back to the surface.

So, you go through the same steps backwards, but with a very important difference: every time you move from one step to the next you say to yourself: "I am moving backwards now **and**, at the same time, I am keeping this nice (or 'pleasurable', as you prefer) sensation of happiness spread all over my body" and off you go to the next step.

You say to yourself the same thing every time you are moving backwards: as a result, when you open your eyes, the nice sensation of happiness will still be there, spread all over your body.

***The Vivid Visualisation Exercise (VVE).***

The purpose of this technique is to enable you to deal appropriately with potentially stressful events or difficult situations that you know you will face in the near future. I suggest you practise it, once or twice a day, in the period of time before the event.

The technique consists of four consecutive steps:

a) first, sit somewhere comfortably and practise for a few minutes the Basic Body Relaxation (BBR);

b) then, keeping your eyes closed, you visualise yourself doing all the things that you would normally do just before the event, in a very relaxed fashion (i.e. if you are concerned about an exam or a job presentation scheduled for 10 am, you see yourself waking up, having breakfast, showering, getting dressed, going out, walking into your office and sitting at your desk), this is the 'before step';

c) now, you visualise yourself going through the event in a very relaxed, comfortable and confident manner, this is the 'during step';

d) finally, you congratulate yourself for the way you have handled the event and, if this is the case, you consider how you can further improve your behaviour or performance, this is the 'after step'.

How can this technique help you? Well, it utilises the wonderful power of our brain to make associations.

Normally, we would associate an event with a sensation or feeling, which could be pleasant or unpleasant (i.e. a piece of music or a song may remind you of your first love or your first slow dance, thus eliciting a pleasant response; or a loud noise may trigger the memory of a car crash).

This time, we use the same power but the other way around: that is, we associate a preceding mood with a current event, because the practice of the VVE will train your brain to associate being calm, comfortable and relaxed when going through a particular event.

A tip I would suggest is that you include in the 'before step' a routine you are very familiar with, something that you know will happen before the event and that you will find easy to visualise: getting off to a good start can significantly improve the efficacy of this technique!

I could offer you plenty of examples of how practising the VVE has helped many of my clients: we go from panic attacks caused by certain situations (i.e. travelling by tube or by plane, or taking a lift), to events such as exams, functions and presentations.

The first example which springs to mind is the case of a bright and talented young professional who was holding back his career because of his fear of speaking in public. This would prevent him from giving presentations which would have dramatically improved his professional standing within his company.

He made the best possible use, through regular practice, of all three steps of the VVE technique visualising himself, first, going through the morning routine at home in a very relaxed fashion; then, dealing with a presentation in a calm and confident manner; finally, congratulating himself, while, at the same time, considering how he could have improved his performance the next time around.

This latter step provided a very useful feedback. Given that one of the triggers for his lack of confidence was the fear of being asked questions he would not know the answer to – though he was very knowledgeable in his area of expertise – he introduced at the start of his presentation an initial statement where he would say:

*"Thank you for giving me the opportunity to present this (indicating the topic). I would welcome your questions and requests for further information. In the likely event (smiling) I would not know the answer to your questions at present, here are my contact details (he*

*would either write on the flip chart his phone number and email address, or have the details indicated on the presentation info-pack), please feel free to get in touch and I will get back to you."*

By saying the above, he was then able to begin the presentation in a much more relaxed and confident manner.

Activities Box 6.

Time for your *PAL …*
*Think about how you would connect with happy feelings in the past and note down similarities and differences.*

and for your *BIT.*
*Practise the PA regularly, at least once a week. Learning how to take care of yourself is just like learning a language (in this case, the language of your emotional self).*

# Chapter 4
# Thoughts

*"Good-humoured patience is necessary with mischievous children and your own mind."*

*Robert Aitkin Roshi*

## Seventh Step
## Exploring the association between thought and language

If I could open a tiny window in people's heads and spring-clean away their emotional ghosts and rational worries in just 2 minutes, I would have a 20-mile long queue outside my office, day and night, all year around.

In reality, I am not able to do that myself, but I can teach you how to do it by yourself, in the next few steps.

You are about to learn three different ways of approaching your concerns (the Language Point, the 3As and the Slide Show Technique), which make up the next three steps of your journey.

***The Fight or Flight Response.***

The Language Point is about talking to ourselves and to others in a healthy and helpful way.

Before I show you how to do that, it is important to appreciate how unhealthy and self-defeating are some common expressions we use in our everyday life and why it would be appropriate to replace them with useful ones.

In order to understand the extent of the damage we cause to ourselves, let's, therefore, first clarify what the 'fight or flight response' is and why it does matter.

In the early 1960s, the American physician Walter Cannon introduced the concept of the 'fight or flight response' when referring to the following basic human biological process and associated behaviour.

When we are confronted with a dangerous and potentially life threatening situation, our body gets ready to fight or flee. It does that by increasing our heartbeat, raising our blood pressure, pumping blood to the appropriate muscles and releasing adrenal hormones. After the fight or the run, as a result of having fought or fled, our body gets back to its natural balance (i.e. slower heart beat and breathing pace).

Now, in the old days, a few hundred thousand years ago, humans were faced with the choice of fighting or fleeing for a number of very simple and basic reasons (predators, hostile tribes, shortage of food supply or routine hunting) and they had plenty of opportunities to elicit the biological response and to get back to a position of balance after the fight or the run. What about us?

Whether we like it or not, we haven't changed much over the past few hundred thousand years, apart from a bit of body hair left behind in our caves (we can do without it in our comfortable and heated homes). This means that when we **perceive** a situation, or a life's event as threatening, we still have the same biological response and still feel the need to release the energy produced and the tension accumulated. The challenge is how to do this in an appropriate way. In other words, can we respond to our contemporary stressors like our ancestors, by fighting or fleeing?

If you are attending a meeting where the closure of your company's business is being discussed, with the prospect of many employees – including yourself – being made redundant in the near future, would you start punching and kicking the hell out of your managers or would you jump and run away?

If you left it to the very last day and the very last moment to pay a bill and you had the brilliant idea of going down to the post office or the bank during your lunch break because the rest of the day you are fully booked and you find a very long queue, would you start knocking down all the people in front of you or would you flee the scene?

As you can see, although we do experience very high levels of stress, as a result of how we perceive our reality, nowadays we find it more difficult to release that energy and tension in such a way that it would not harm anybody, including ourselves. So, some people *explode,* turning against their fellow humans verbally (i.e. shouting, insulting), mentally (hating, plotting), or physically (smashing furniture, slapping, punching), while others *implode,* turning against themselves (depression, compulsive behaviours, anxiety attacks, eating disorders).

Now that we know what is going on, what can we do about it? Well, we can, on the one hand, learn how to avoid putting pressure on ourselves, to minimise the release of stress hormones, and, on the other, we can learn how to release appropriately the tension, once it is already there.

***The Language Point.***

There are two categories of words that would be appropriate to delete from our vocabulary: the imperatives and the self-defeating.

The imperatives are expressions like: *I must*, *I should*, *I have to*, *I ought to*, *this is urgent*. Every time we say them, we place a weight on our shoulders. Every time we pronounce them, we colour in a particular way our reality, perceiving life's events not just as they are but in a darker and more powerful light.

This triggers a fight or flight biological response with all the consequences seen above.

If you are in the habit of using imperatives on a daily basis, imagine how much damage this has caused to your physical, emotional and rational components, as a whole, over the past few years.

Self-defeating words are expressions like: *I cannot* and *I need*. Every time we say them we corner ourselves facing a huge wall of our own making.

If you cannot, you cannot, what else can you do? If you need, you need, how else can you go about it? Do you see how disempowering these expressions are? If you are normally using these words, do you see how much damage this has caused to your self-esteem, day after day, week after week, over the past few years?

How can we rephrase imperatives and self-defeating expressions?

Let's start from the imperatives. You may use them on two occasions: personal life or professional life's events. If you are using them to refer to personal life events (i.e. "I must go to the gym", "I have to eat healthily", etc.), you are advised to replace them with preferences (i.e. "I would like to", "I would love to", "it would be great", "it would be interesting", "it would be useful").

As a practical example, I offer you the experience of a young lady who came to me complaining of her dissatisfaction with her body.

She had used comfort eating as a way of addressing her emotional issues and, as a result, she had put on considerable weight, which was now causing added distress.

Every morning she would have her exercise-bag ready for the gym and every morning she would say to herself, literally, "come on now, you stupid bitch, you must go to the gym" or "you silly cow, today there are no excuses, you have to go to the gym".

Bearing in mind that the gym was located in the basement of her office building and that the fees were subsidised by her company, it really looked like it would have been so easy for her to go, so why didn't she manage to get there?

Well, now you too are aware of how there were two powerful forces in action here. The first was the reaction caused by her using imperatives in an attempt to convince herself to go to the gym. The imperatives caused a lot of pressure, which in her case easily teamed up with anxiety.

Humans are pleasure seeking creatures and having a choice, we would rather pass on something associated with anxiety and procrastinate than engage with it, and that's what she did.

The second was the reaction caused by her bad-mouthing herself. The inner adult was reproaching the inner child too forcefully and the resulting reaction was equally powerful.

Imagine you are standing still and, at the same time, one person is pulling your right arm and another one is pulling your left arm, which way would you go?

You are stuck there, not free to move either way and, in the process, this also hurts. That was exactly the place where this lady was when she came to see me.

My answer was simple and clear: stop fighting with yourself. It's a war lost from the start and, though it may look like you are winning a few battles now and then, in the end there will be no winners and only one loser: you.

How to go about it, then? Make peace with yourself. Treat yourself nicely, gently and with respect. Listen to your inner adult and, at the same time, let your inner child play. I introduced her to Artemíology and the Language Point.

How did it go with the gym? As soon as she replaced imperatives with "I enjoy going to the gym" or "I would like to go to the gym, because it makes me feel better" she started exercising regularly for not less than three times a week.

How do you rephrase imperatives when you apply them to study or work situations?

Here, of course, the use of preferences does not seem appropriate. In real life most people – though they may like their jobs and find them interesting or stimulating – are not really in love with their profession and having a choice they would rather do something else with their time.

So, let's use as an example a typical sentence, which can be easily adapted to your own circumstances: "I must complete this report by the end of the week."

First, let's note how unhealthy the above sentence is. When we use the expression "I must" not only may we trigger the fight or flight biological response, whose associated natural behaviours would clash with our professional duty, but we also start off by putting ourselves in a victim situation. "I must…poor me…this is unfair…why should I?" The above sentence allows no boundaries between who we are, as persons, what we do for a living, at this given time in our life, and the task in hand. This means that we totally identify ourselves – and our sense of self-worth – with the job we do and how we perform in this specific task.

This way, if we perform 7 out of 10, we are more likely to feel unhappy or concerned about not having reached a full result than to be happy about having achieved 7.

We are more than what we do for a living during a given time of our life and much more than a single – though very important – task.

When we talk to ourselves like this, we create a black hole, which inevitably sucks in who we are and the very reasons why we are doing what we are doing with our life.

The likely consequence of talking like that will be to procrastinate and wait until the very last moment to get the report done, which naturally does not help improve the quality of our work.

In such cases, we may use virtually anything to reduce the anxiety caused by the way we perceive our situation ("I must…") and we may end up tiding up a desk which had not been given any attention for the past three years and could have waited, at least, a few more weeks, or sorting computer files that had never attracted our attention since their original creation.

Let's see how just some minor but significant changes can turn an unhealthy sentence into a helpful one. I would like you to rephrase the sentence like this: "I know that my current (or present) goal is to complete this report by the end of the week."

Noticed the differences? Well, first of all, you are not saying "I must…" you are saying "I know…" In your mind this is the equivalent of walking upright rather than walking with a heavy weight on your shoulders or dragging around an iron ball chained to your ankle.

When you say "I know" you associate yourself with your resources, with all that you know and studied or trained for, rather than connecting with your doubts and fears.

Then you say "that my current goal is to complete…", and this helps you see the event for what it really is: that you are a person who has decided to carry out a given course of studies or profession, which entails the completion of specific tasks. This allows the creation of healthy boundaries between who you are and what you do for a living, which are essential for building and keeping up your self-esteem.

If you talked to yourself like this you are more likely to carry out your given tasks and also more likely to perform better. You are also more likely to contribute to the improvement of your work procedures or environment, because you will be able to put forward sound reasons to justify the changes and motivate your colleagues and managers.

How do we rephrase self-defeating expressions like “I cannot” and “I need”?

Well, the latter can be rephrased exactly like you do with the imperatives. The former, instead, can be replaced by using the relevant adjective.

You see, each time we say “I cannot”, we corner ourselves into a situation where there is no way out but retreating. Imagine yourself facing the corner of your room and walking towards it. At some point you will stop, otherwise you will bang your head on the wall. If you go right or left, you hit the wall, so the only way out is going backwards.

This is exactly what happens in your mind when you say “I cannot”. You take your brain to a very frustrating place. The answer is: say what you mean. In reality, 99.9% of the time you mean:

I find this extremely difficult, or
I find this very difficult, or
I find this quite difficult, or
I find this fairly difficult, or
I find this difficult.

The difference is that when you use any of the above, from the most powerful (extremely) to the less forceful (just difficult), you are not cornering your brain and your mind will be more likely to suggest ways to go around or beneath your hurdle.

I could give you many examples of how practising the Language Point has improved the life of many of my clients. The first case that springs to mind, which is also the last in chronological order, is that of a young lady suffering from bulimia whose comment was:

*"Tommaso, look, when I first heard you talking about this I thought 'what a nonsense... this is bullshit... I don't believe I am here listening to this man'. Then I decided to take your word for it, after all I had nothing to lose and there was no harm in trying, if only to come back to you in two weeks' time and tell you in your face what crap this whole thing was. But, now...I don't know how to put this...I believe this thing actually works. I know it's early days, but I feel that there is so much I can do to help myself, whereas in the past I would carry on thinking only about all the things I could not do".*

My tips about how to go about practising the language point are: the sooner you start practising the language point the better.

However, go with the flow and don't put pressure on yourself. It will take some time for you to re-adjust to a new healthy way of talking to yourself and to others, don't be in a hurry.

When you realise that you have just used an imperative or a self-defeating word, don't beat yourself up. To the contrary, congratulate yourself for having been able to spot the difference and rephrase the expression. You are not competing against someone else. Do not compete against yourself.

I have started practising the language point in January 2000 and now, in those rare occasions when an unhealthy word like "I need" or "I cannot" slips through, first, I realise how just the sound of it clashes with my internal state, then I spontaneously smile, and, finally, I rephrase it, saying what I mean.

Activities Box 7.

Time for your *PAL* ...
*Think about the fight and flight response. What are the similarities and differences that you find between our life as humans a few hundred thousand years ago and now.*

and for your *BIT*.
*Start practising the Language Point.*

## Eighth Step
## Dealing with negative thoughts

**The 3As.**

The 3As technique can help you deal with negative thoughts. The three As stand for:

- ✓ Acknowledgement
- ✓ Awareness
- ✓ Action

First, let's see what meaning we attach to the above words, and then, I will give you an example of how this exercise can be applied to a real life situation. Please note that, where possible, I would recommend carrying out this exercise in writing.

The **acknowledgement** step answers the question "what is this all about?" This step gives you the opportunity to recollect precisely what has triggered your negative thinking (i.e. an abusive phone call from an ex-partner, an inappropriate comment from a colleague, the sudden illness of a dear friend, etc.).

I have found in my professional experience that clients at times sink deep down into a spiral of negative thoughts as a result of something that they have genuinely misheard, misinterpreted or misconstrued.

In such instances, it is not a case of actually dealing with a difficult or problematic negative event, rather it is about acknowledging that our misperception of what happened at that time had tricked us into believing that we heard something when something else had been said.

Naturally, the best way to go about this step would be to ask our interlocutor to clarify their point (i.e. "did I hear you correctly when you said…?"). When this is not feasible, going back to notes taken at the time may help, or reading again the letter or email that caused our distress in the first place.

Failing all of the above, just write down what you think has happened. It is important to note that what you are doing here is not analysing yourself or the situation, but, rather, just observing it.

The **awareness** step answers in three ways the question "why has this happened?" In the English language the terms *acknowledgement* and *awareness* may at times be used as synonyms.

In the context of this technique, they have a different meaning: the awareness step is deeper and more connected with higher rational processes than the initial acknowledgment one. Here you ask yourself three questions:

- *Why do I think this has happened?*
  This is your own interpretation of the event.

- *What a third party might think about what has happened? (if nobody else was present at the time or you don't feel it would be appropriate to ask, what do you think a camera would have seen?)*
  This is the account provided by a friend or a colleague, or an explanation based on your essential description (as if a camera were filming the event).

- *Why would I do or say something like that, if I were this person?*

This is you focussing on the person who has caused your problem or has triggered your negative thoughts and stepping in their shoes.

The **action** step answers to the question "how to go about this?"

In real life most of us not only don't give ourselves the chance to relax and calm down, like we suggest doing as you go through the practice of the emotional component exercises, but also jump straightaway from thinking a negative thought to performing our (explosive or implosive) response, often in a matter of seconds.

It goes without saying that such actions – or reactions – do not adequately address the issue and, in most cases, actually end up making things worse. If we follow the steps above things can be different, as the following case illustrates.

A young woman came to me complaining about her difficult work situation. She was a dark-haired, very good looking and well-educated Anglo-French lady. She had been working for the same multinational company for a number of years and up to that moment she had been enjoying her job as a personal assistant to one of the directors of the London office.

Her job was well paid and, most importantly, her working hours gave her the opportunity to attend a part-time Master degree course in Business Administration.

She had a very good relationship with her boss, who would value her opinion and discussed regularly work issues with her. Unfortunately, her boss decided to take an early retirement and went back to his country, and the new one did not seem to connect with her at all.

Her professional situation had become such a source of distress that she had thought of resigning from her position. I was her last chance to try to do something about it.

The core of the problem was essentially the way the new boss was treating her. The previous director was a middle-aged Spanish gentleman with impeccable manners and a fine sense of humour, the new one was a young English guy whom she could hardly see in person, as he would get into work before her, leave after her and, above all, communicate with her mostly through internal emails.

The way he gave her directives was driving her nuts: she would find folders piled up on her desk in the morning with brief but detailed instructions typed on A4 sheets of paper. She said: “that jerk does not even have the decency to use the phone!” There was none of the niceties and warm interactions she had with the previous boss and none of the professional discussion where she felt that her experience in the role and her intellectual abilities were valued and utilised.

She suddenly felt downgraded to a role of typist she had never performed even during the early days of her employment within the company.

We agreed to get together for a couple of intensive meetings where I would show her how to take care of her physical and emotional components and then, we would work gradually, step by step, through the exercises of the rational component. When it was time for her to practise the 3As, she offered the following feedback.

Acknowledgment.

*My boss is an arrogant public school boy.*

Awareness.

First why (what did she think herself):
*He looks down on me because I am not English (*she perceived herself more as French*) and because he is a bastard of a man and I am a woman.*

Second why (what did a colleague think of the situation):
The personal assistant to the other director, who shared her large office with her and whose desk was right opposite hers said: "*You may not be aware of the fact that you may come across as a woman with a strong personality and that man looks a bit shy to me. He also seems to be quite young. I bet he comes straight out of University and has had not much practical professional experience, so that's why he is probably avoiding contact with you: he may be afraid of displaying his weaknesses.*"

Third why (what did she think he was thinking):
*She is just a secretary, who cares? I have far more important things to do than wasting time with her, or trying to be nice to her.*

When I asked her to comment on the exercise, she said:

*"Well, as you know before I practised the 3As I thought I had no option but to leave the job. I wrote down in the first why of the awareness step very much what I thought of this guy.*

*Then, when I listened to what my colleague had to say – and got on board the second why – something clicked in the back of my mind.*

*I mean, I was still thinking that he was a jerk, but there could have been one chance in a million that my colleague was right.*

*Up to that moment, my reaction had been to keep it to myself. So, although we have the tradition of ending the working week by meeting down the pub on Friday evenings, I had not been down there since the new director arrived because I just wanted to avoid a big argument or a fight. But, after practising the 3As, something clicked in me and I decided to go down the pub last Friday and check this guy out for myself.*

*From the very first moments I could see my colleague had been right about him. He was nice and very shy and when I got close enough for a one-to-one chat I asked him about his previous working experiences. That was his first important job and before he had been working as a researcher for his university.*

*At that point, I took the courage to ask why he was communicating with me as he was, and I also told him that his behaviour seemed a bit odd to me.*

*He apologised and openly confessed that he didn't mean to be rude and to diminish my role. It was just that he wanted to do his best and this was the first big opportunity he had to show his skills. That's why he would get into work very early in the morning and leave quite late. He wanted to make sure that everything was well organised and planned for the day ahead and he thought that by organising my work load for me, by sorting out my folders and leaving me written notes, he was actually making my life easier."*

The rest of the story goes that from that point on their relationship improved as she felt almost like mothering this young chap in his new important job, and he began asking her for her opinion on professional matters, as well as for a complete course on how to choose appropriate clothes and how to match accessories (i.e. ties, belts and shoes).

The 3As is a simple exercise and not a magical formula. Different techniques work differently for different people. However, I believe that small changes can make a big difference. This is even more true when the small changes we apply to how we perceive ourselves and the world around us are introduced nicely and gradually, and at the appropriate time.

Activities Box 8.

Time for your *PAL* …
*Think about the 3As. How have you been dealing with your negative thoughts so far and what changes might this exercise introduce in the way you appraise an event?*

and for your *BIT.*
*Start practising the 3As.*

# Thoughts

## Ninth Step
## Turning thoughts into resources

The last and, probably, the most important exercise we learn in this chapter is the Slide Show Technique (SST).

The goal of the SST is to help you re-process your thoughts in a healthy, useful and helpful way by turning them into resources.

Up to this point you have been storing the incoming information into two different containers, one for the positive and one for the negative thoughts. The downside of this way of processing and storing thoughts lies in the fact that, sooner or later, the two containers (especially the negative one) become full and than you can hear yourself saying 'I have had enough' or 'I can't take this anymore' or 'this is too much for me'.

We may suffer even more when the negative container becomes full gradually, almost subtly, because the pain and confusion we experience catch us by surprise and because we find it difficult to grasp how the latest negative event, especially if it is a minor thing (the straw that broke the camel's back), can trigger such a response.

Truth is, we don't appreciate how the problem does not lie in the final little negative thought, but with the thousands we had previously allowed to sink in.

What can we do about this? We can leave the hardware as it is and take care of upgrading the software by downloading a new application: the SST.

Practising the SST will change the way you process your thoughts and turn all of them, both negative and positive, into precious resources.

The Language Point has shown you how to prevent placing unnecessary pressure on yourself.

The 3As has provided you with a simple strategy to ensure that you don't make a mountain out of a molehill.

The Slide Show Technique will enable you to re-process all the rubbish already stored in your system and, at the same time, will help you change the processing system itself, making sure that you don't keep on storing rubbish in the future.

Now, let me ask you just one question, before I show you how to go about the SST. When does your new day start? I don't mean this in an existential, philosophical way. I mean, a normal, ordinary day.

When you get up in the morning? It may look like it, but no…try again. When you wake up? No. When you have your breakfast? No. When you have your shower? No. When you get dressed and walk out of your house? No. When you get into your office? No.

The answer is: you start a new day soon after you have closed the day before.

Now, how many of you manage to close your day? Bear in mind that there are three components to ourselves and you want to reset all three of them (physical, emotional and rational). If you don't reset your system, by appropriately closing the previous day, you will not be able to start a new day, you will be simply carrying on the day (and week, and month, and year) before. That's why we come to a point when we say: "I have had enough!"

So, for example, when you have a late supper (with or without lots of drinks) and then you plunge into bed without allowing enough time for digesting your food, you are very likely to have poor sleep, get up in the morning not feeling rested (and maybe not even wanting to leave the bed!) and with a foul taste in your mouth.

As a result, you are very likely to skip breakfast and end up at work like a zombie: your stomach empty, your mind in bed and your body wandering around the office. This is how you do not start your new day, but rather carry your previous one forward, physiologically.

The same applies when you don't make peace with yourself emotionally (remember the BBR, IB and 3BS exercises?) and carry forward emotions belonging to one day to the next, like sweeping under the carpet a little dust every day until the day when you trip, fall over and hit your head as a result of the big bumps you have created under the carpet.

The same also applies when you don't take the time to reflect on your rational concerns and you create monsters of *Worry* out of negative thoughts not addressed at the appropriate time.

My point is: in order to deal appropriately with our issues, we want to make sure that we close our day, every day, thus resetting the whole of our system by allowing our brain to carry out its maintenance job and take care of our physiological hitches, emotional issues and rational concerns.

Now, let's first see how to practise this exercise and then we will add some final comments.

**The Slide Show Technique (SST).**

It would be useful to practise a bit of BBR and IB before starting the SST. When you find yourself seated comfortably somewhere with your eyes closed and you become aware of your state of relaxation, you may start taking the following steps:

1. Think about a slide show and imagine how you would like to create yours. For example, are your slides coming in your visual field from the right and going out to the left or the other way around, or perhaps you prefer visualising them coming in from the top or the bottom, or flashing in and out – like the slides in a Power point presentation. Once you have decided your chosen motion you can move to the next step.

2. Ask yourself: "has anything meaningful (or interesting) happened today?" If nothing comes up, you practise the 3Bs and you are done. If more items come up, you just pick one of them and work through it, as indicated below.

3. Allow the item to come in your visual field, like a slide in a slide show. Visualise it as clearly as possible. It doesn't matter if the slide is in black & white, colour or 3D, as long as you have a clear visualisation any format is fine.

4. Ask yourself: "how do I feel about this event? Is this item positive (i.e. a

colleague paying you a compliment) or negative? (i.e. a difficult meeting with a former friend)."

5. Now you want to consolidate your appreciation of this event as positive or negative by 'framing' it as positive or negative. You can do this by visualising yourself writing on the top of the slide with a pen or with your finger a plus (+), or a minus ( - ) sign, or writing 'positive' or 'negative', or using a colour which, like an aura, goes around the slide (i.e. there was a lady who would visualise a tubular neon sign going around the slide and the sign turned black for negative and orange for positive).

6. Next, ask yourself: "what can I learn from this?" Please note that this question is not future oriented. It is a simple question designed, among other things, to make sure that you are able to make peace with yourself and reset your system. So, we are not asking the question to elicit any deep philosophical revelation or to find the solution to one of the endemic problems afflicting humanity. Just go with the flow, be happy with everything you get with

this exercise and don't vet what your mind is bringing up to the surface (i.e. don't say things like "this item is too trivial to be worked through let's fish another one", or "this answer is too simple, let's think of something more intelligent"). Humans have developed on this planet thanks to their extraordinary capacity to make sense of things and learn from them. So, don't worry. Be there, calm and relaxed, and you will see that one or more answers will come to you.

7. Now that you know that you have learnt something from this particular positive or negative event, it is time to reframe it as a learning experience. To do that, say to yourself in your mind: "now that I have learnt this (and you name what you have learnt), this event has become a learning experience" and you consolidate this by visualising yourself first brushing off the previous positive or negative framing and then writing on the top of your slide either a symbol of your choice (i.e. a diamond, a star, an asterisk, etc.) if you used a symbol (+ or -) to frame the slide before, or if you wrote 'positive' or 'negative' you can now write 'learning experience'

on its top. If you used a colour around the slide, you can now choose a new colour (the lady of the example before had her neon sign turning green).

8. The event you have been dealing with has become a learning experience. It is not a positive or negative item anymore. Now that you have washed away its unhealthy charge and unhelpful connotation, you can let it slide away from your visual field and into your storage system. You can go back and see if there is any other meaningful (or interesting) thing, which has happened during the day, and work through it the same way.

So, what happens to items when you let them go? They are not negative anymore, so they won't go in the negative container and they are not positive anymore, so they won't go in the positive container.

Truth is, our brain has already a nice chest of drawers ready for it, where items are stored by topics rather than by charge and connotation.

This is the software upgrade I was referring to at the beginning of this step. Your system had been ready for it since birth, but you had never used this advanced option so far. There are drawers for all sorts of items and topics. The beautiful thing is: topics will never come back from the past to haunt you – as negative thoughts, like ghosts, can do – topics are resources that will spring to mind only to make you feel better.

What happens to the material already stored in our containers? As I said, your brain will recognise immediately that you are using its most advanced application and, as you keep on practising the SST every day, it will gradually convert items previously stored in the bins into topics and store them in the relevant drawer.

I warmly recommend that you practise the SST on a daily basis. When? Whenever it suits you. Some practise as soon as they are back at home in the evening, some after supper or before going to bed, others on the train as they commute back home from work.

What happens if you forget or skip one day? Nothing really. It is easier and healthier to deal with your issues on a daily basis. If you skip one day the following day you will work on two days rather than one.

When you get into the habit of closing your day, every day, wonderful little things will happen to you and I'm talking about those little things that make your life worth living.

Also, the next time life throws at you something unpleasant, you are more likely to say: "hum, hang on a moment, I have been here before and I know what to do..." making use of your experience and connecting with your rational resources, rather than sinking in a downward negative spiral and saying: "oh, dear here it goes again...how can I go about it now?...why is this happening to me now? ... it's all happening now, am I cursed, or something?"

At this point you may ask: "Look, we can see why it would be useful to get rid of the negative container, but why do you want to get rid of the positive one too? Wouldn't it be nice to keep the positive bin?"

You see, this is when we face the transition from theory to practice. Useful theories help us improve our real life and the old two-bins system is not doing us any favour. I have seen clients suffering considerable psychological pain as a result of having their positive bins filled up. How is this possible?

These persons had lost the capacity to look forward, the drive to live their lives because they were living in their past, all immersed in cuddling their happy memories.

They began isolating themselves from friends and family and fell first into a state of pleasurable numbness, then into a condition where they were not able to tell anymore which dimension was real, the one they had in their mind or the one they had around them.

Their positive bin had become a powerful magnet, which – just like a black hole – was sucking in their vital energy, disconnecting these persons from their present and future.

When we practise the SST we don't simply get rid of the positive bin, we convert it into a precious and more advanced resource system, which we will be using as a helpful ally throughout our life.

I often use the following metaphor when I introduce the SST to my clients.

Imagine you have bought a ticket for a theatre performance. You walk in the theatre, take your seat and wait for the play to begin. After some forty minutes the curtains are still down and no sign of the actors. You begin feeling a bit nervous. Twenty minutes later you hear voices and noises coming from the stage but the curtains are still down. You start wondering what is going on. Twenty minutes later the curtains are still down. You may begin arguing with the person sitting next to you, you may start shouting in protest, you may pick a fight with somebody, or you may stay seated in your chair thinking about it or writing about it. You may blame yourself for being there, or for being faulty or stupid, because you don't understand what's going on.

You may also think that you are the only one who understands what is happening: you may believe that it is a new alternative form of theatre you are viewing, one which asks the public to imagine what's happening behind the curtains and make their own representations in their minds about how life is on the other side. After all, you do hear noises and voices coming from there, don't you?

Well, whether you like it or not. This is a metaphor of your life. You get here, take your place and would like to enjoy the show. You won't be fully able to do so until you lift the curtains (or somebody else does it for you).

The two huge dichotomies-curtains (positive and negative, good and bad, right and wrong) are preventing you from connecting with real life, with what is being performed on the stage.

You have a choice: carry out one or more of the behaviours shown in my example or lift the curtains and make a new start.

Once the curtains are up everything is possible.

You may decide to sit down, relax and enjoy the show. You may wish to join in the performance in a variety of ways (i.e. as a main actor, an extra, a member of the technical team, a musician, etc.). You may choose to do something this side of the stage (i.e. selling ice cream, assisting disabled persons getting in and out of the theatre, etc.). Once the curtains are up you can see clearly and real life may begin.

The SST upgrade makes a difference in our lives because it frees us from the shackles of the dichotomies: positive and negative, good or bad, right or wrong. It allows us to walk upright, as humans deserve to, focusing on what is healthy, useful and helpful.

Activities Box 9.

Time for your *PAL* …
*Think about the SST. Have you ever closed your day in the past? If you have, how did you go about it and what differences do you find in the SST's way of doing it?*

and for your *BIT*.
*Start practising the SST on a daily basis.*

Yes, prayer & thinking about positives of the day before I sleep but not thinking of negatives nor of the learning experience.

# Second Part

# Levels, Behaviours & Time Perspectives

# Chapter 5
# Opinions

*"Know thyself."*

*Taletes (630BC)*

## Tenth Step
## The intrapersonal level

Practising the first nine steps of this guide will have helped distance yourself from unhealthy habits, negative feelings and rational concerns. However, one of the core messages of Artemíology is that learning is a life long process and learning to take care of yourself is no exception.

We learn through experience and we experience through learning and, in so doing, we enrich ourselves personally and professionally as time goes by.

Now that you are in a safer place, you don't want to go back to where you were before. The three steps that make up this chapter will show you how to stay in this healthy, useful and helpful place for as long as you wish.

We are often too hard on ourselves and we take life too seriously. However, the more you know about how you function and respond to different situations, the more relaxed you will be about your life's choices and events. Therefore, don't be afraid of getting to know who you are.

Before I show you how to travel within yourself to discover who you really are, I think it would be useful to take first a closer look at what kind of society we live in. This will help us appreciate the powerful forces we interact with as we go about our daily routines.

The interaction between ourselves and our environment originates our personal conditions (i.e. happiness or sadness). Our capacity for dealing with the above interaction is strongly impaired by what I would define as '***the disguising factor***'.

By disguising factor I mean the basic fact that our consumer society, by marketing resources as needs, in its pursuit of increasing the occasions and opportunities for our shopping, reduces us to a confused state, which may easily trigger unhealthy behaviours.

Let us take food, as an example. The primary importance of food is its nutritional value. The secondary aspects of food are: its taste, its look and the rapidity with which you can eat it.

Consumer society wants us to eat more than our body would ever need – in terms of nutritional requirements – so it bombards us with adverts that emphasise all the secondary appealing aspects of food. The result: we are eating too many saturated fats, sugars and processed stuff, thus creating the conditions for our poor physical health.

Consumer society treats us like idiots, who are 'valued' for their spending power rather than for their intellectual, emotional or spiritual faculties. Consumer society's motto is: "shop until you drop."

Artemíology's motto is: "care until you share."

The good news is that it is never too late to learn and change. Truth is, human behaviours do not simplistically follow the physical law of cause and effect and a single behaviour may originate from a complex mix of internal and external factors.

That's where getting to know who you are comes in. By becoming fully aware of your present strengths and weaknesses, you will be in a position to consolidate the former and work on the latter.

First of all, create some time for yourself (a few slots of at least 30 minutes each during the next few days, better if not on consecutive days) and follow the steps below.

Begin each time your self-exploration activities with the BBR, the IB and the 3Bs. Close each time your activities with the 3Bs or the 3Bs + the PA.

1. On the first day, write down a list made of ten "I am…" statements (i.e. "I am a good listener", "I am a lousy dancer"). Jot them down without over-analysing them. Go with the flow. Write the first things coming up and do not change the statements once you have written them down. Place this list in a folder and somewhere safe.

2. On the second day, write a second "I am…" list, without looking at the first list. Then, write down another list made

of a minimum of ten things that you value in yourself.

3. On the third day, write a third “I am…” list, without looking at the previous ones. Then, write down another list made of the things that you see as your weaknesses.

4. On the fourth day, write a fourth “I am…” list, without looking at the previous ones. Then, write down another list made of the things that you like about your current situation.

5. On the fifth day, write a fifth “I am…” list, without looking at the previous ones. Then, write down another list made of the things that you dislike about your current situation.

6. On the sixth day, write a sixth “I am…” list, without looking at the previous ones. Then, write down another list made of the things that make you happy (i.e. the things that you find interesting or pleasurable which you would like to do in your leisure time).

7. On the seventh day, write a seventh "I am..." list, without looking at the previous ones. Then, write down another list made of the things that don't make you happy.

8. On the eighth day, you calmly read aloud the seven "I am..." lists. Then, reflect on what you have written and if you notice any meaningful changes from the first list to the last one. Finally, make a list of the things you believe in.

9. On the ninth day, you calmly read aloud all the other lists. Then, reflect on what you have written. What do they say about you?

***One story, many lives.***

I think it could be useful to offer now a letter written to me by a lady I had seen a few years ago. I believe many of you will identify themselves, partially or totally, with her experience.

*My Story*

*I began my search almost 15 years ago, maybe longer now. I had no idea at the time that my search would lead me to a consulting room in central London.*

*One of the first questions I was asked was: "What do you want out of this?" It only took me a small moment to reply: "Peace".*

*I had become a non-person. I was numb and disconnected from life and living. I had grown up with many responsibilities. I had become dedicated to everyone else's needs and concerns. I was always on my best behaviour and did everything I was told. The last thing I wanted was to cause more dis-ease in our lives. Of course these responsibilities were placed on me by myself. I discovered later, that they gave me purpose and made me feel needed and valued.*

*So I became a little adult at the age of 7 or so. Everything I did or touched I had to succeed at. I gave everything my best by challenging and disciplining my 'self' all of the time. I was very hard on my 'self' yet very empathic and forgiving of others. I was never good enough, never strong enough, too female, too weak, not intelligent enough and unsatisfactory.*

*These words became my mantra. They became my focus, my drive. They encouraged me to go harder, faster, deeper. I lived by their energy and their energy alone. I imagined I was a racehorse, training for racing perfection.*

*It is amazing how I had nurtured these thoughts to punish myself and it was never enough. I had managed to turn all of my external chaos inwardly and blame myself. I was condemned.*

*The more power I gave to my mantra the more I was becoming disconnected from my family, my friends, my dreams, my passions and me. This focus at the beginning had protected me and cocooned me. It had kept me busy accomplishing.*

*I was always away from the house, at school, at ballet, at competitive swimming, at gymnastics and part time jobs. I kept time racing, so I wouldn't have to stop and think. I was constantly on the move never resting in one place for long. I was wearing a life jacket, but not just for emergencies, I was wearing it permanently.*

*My life jacket was a protective barrier from the world, it wasn't saving me, my life jacket was drowning me.*

*Before I knew it, I was lost. I knew no other way. The accomplishments had become constant punishments. The achievements were never satisfactory. The rewards were empty and people's compliments were hollow. I heard nothing and tasted nothing. I was dead.*

*My 'unlearning' was the most difficult exercise I ever undertook, but because of that fact, I took it up as my new challenge. I gave it one thousand per cent, dedicating all my energies to it. The reality of having to sit down and be honest to another human being was petrifying. I was thrown from being totally committed to the project to wanting to completely abandon it. I was in, and then I was out. I was tuned in, and then turned off.*

*My energies had to be re-trained and re-focused. They were not ready for the new territory in which they needed to belong in order for me to survive. My feelings were threatened; they were comfortable where they were. They were content and understood their domain. I had to build them a new house and they did not want to move in. They were quite comfortable living the way they were.*

*My entire world was being viewed from another window of the same house. Essentially, I had to learn to trust that good would come to me, that I was not being punished and that my life was a worthy one. I had to take a step forward.*

*The first thing I remember that made me listen was a simple question, which I asked myself: "Do you want to live or do you want to die?" "If you continue this way we will find you dead lying by the toilet." This was my trigger. It shot through my numbness and jolted me awake.*

*The truth I have learned is painful. I have learned that life is hard. I have learned that to live is to feel. I have learned to cry and to laugh, to be sad and to feel joy. I realised that I had long been dead but now I am alive. I feel.*

*I would encourage everyone to take a risk and discover the hidden parts of you that you have long trained into submission. They are part of you. They need to be cherished and understood. You cannot escape them. They have unbounded wisdom and will find a way to show themselves eventually. In order to be at peace, I needed to listen to all of me.*

*My life has become rich. I have become a lover, a sister, an aunty, and a daughter. I am learning new things every day. At the beginning my voices were like thunder in my head. Sometimes the rain clouds break again, pouring all over me, but somehow they don't wet me like they used to. I now treasure these opportunities to continue my growth. Now, I can say: "I am at peace."*

Activities Box 10.

Time for your *PAL …*
*Carry out the self-exploration activities above.*

and for your *BIT.*
*Discuss the outcome of your self-exploration activities with one of your friends.*

# Chapter 6
# Choices

*"Be true to yourself in what you do with your life."*

*Aristotle*

## Eleventh Step
## The personal level

Now that you know yourself a bit better, it is time to put this knowledge to good use and see how you can improve the quality of your personal life. As a start let's consider how the social environment we live in impacts on the personal choices we make by introducing what I would define as '***the speed factor***'.

As the German sociologist Bernd Guggenberger notes: *"We live as forgetful beings under the spell of speed, we carry on as if we were always travelling and bringing with us the absolute minimum required in terms of tradition, affection and personal identity. We have become 'chameleons of ethics' leaving behind great passions and high ideals because they were the cause of difficulties and pathos.*

*In the celebration of the 'here and now', feelings, like fashion, are quickly born and rapidly fade away. Qualities are not to be really possessed, but effectively shown: there is no time to discover and evaluate them, that would require a long relationship, so we relate to others merely on the basis of how they appear to be."*

Bellino also observes how: *"The overwhelming rapidity of social change (Goethe's 'Das Veloziferische') has originated not only the crisis of ideologies, but the crisis of our personal planning capacity, too."*

Incredibly high rhythms of personal life within a rapidly changing social environment inevitably take their toll on our physical and psychological wellbeing. Our species has become what it is as a result of millions of years of evolution and it has had no time to catch up with what has happened in the past 150 years – that is, an insignificantly short time, in evolutionary terms.

Try to imagine how our life was in 1865. How many sources of stress and anxiety can you think of? Can you hear your office telephones ringing, or the trills originated by the mobile phone in your pocket?

Can you hear the noise coming from busy streets and the roar of car engines while you are waiting at the bus stop? Can you enjoy healthy breathing within a packed underground train or the comforting view of the evening news flooding your auditory channels with information whose quality is finely matched by the stuff they are making us eat and bravely call 'food'?

The past 150 years have severely put us to the test, and the speed factor, with its deep and far-reaching implications for our physical and psychological health, has been largely underestimated by mainstream psychology, which has mostly been concerned with relieving some of its effects (i.e. stress, anxiety) rather than with confronting their sources.

The stress you suffer as a result of the sheer speed at which you live is often made worse by the tendency of companies towards downsizing their job force. Losing a job is not just stressful for those who actually lose it. Those who are left behind feel the added pressure of knowing that they have been spared this time around and often work more, as fewer employees now deal with the same workload. Those still employed bear also the extra worry that there could be more layoffs in the future, which is even worst, psychologically, than knowing for sure that they will indeed lose their job in a given time in the future.

In such circumstances, it is not uncommon that people are drawn towards extreme personal and professional choices, like leaving everything behind and escaping somewhere else – often as a consequence of a nervous break down – or throwing themselves even more into their professional activities, thus leaving virtually no room for their personal life.

Coming up with balanced practical alternatives becomes naturally difficult in these situations. However, embracing the challenge of making our life a better place within our present environment represents, in almost all cases, the only sensible way forward.

Here is a step-by-step indication of how you can go about your personal orientation activity:

1. First, choose somebody you trust and whose opinion you value. In the end, you

will be the one to decide how to go about your personal issues, but it does help to have somebody to talk to. Sometimes good ideas come up as a result of interacting with the appropriate person.

2. Then, start looking after your body by:

    a) Making a little time for yourself every day (i.e. leisure time, friends and family).

    b) Slowing down the pace of your daily activities. Practising regularly the BBR will help you do this.

    c) Begin exercising nicely and gently every day (even room exercises will do).

3. Next, nurture your emotional self by connecting with each moment of your day. Live fully every little thing that you do. Practising the IB and the 3Bs can help you do this.

4. Finally, give a boost to your rational self by living as a 'special' person. The exercises carried out during the previous

step, where you gave yourself the opportunity to know more about who you are, can be put to use now. Special persons live a special life, one that is full of special things. You know what you like and what makes you happy, so go for it!

Another important issue worth addressing here is the close association between the personal choices you make and how happy you are with your professional life.

I have worked with many clients whose personal life was pretty ok, but whose dissatisfaction with their job brought about considerable suffering and often triggered unhealthy behaviours (i.e. vomiting, drinking) or unwanted conditions (i.e. loss of sleep, bad temper).

In such cases, I would advise creating some time to re-think your career and think about your professional orientation. To help you do that, you may follow the step-by-step guidance offered below. The goal of the following activity is to come up with a grid whose fully completed version will provide you with a clear indication of your career aspirations.

I strongly recommend you to carry out this activity, step-by-step, exactly as it is indicated. This is because even the slightest tendency towards jumping to conclusions and predicting the outcome of the next step would compromise the usefulness of this exercise.

Please note that two sample professional orientation grids are provided in Appendix C and D. The first is blank, the second is fully completed and scored.

This is how to complete your **professional orientation** grid:

1. Make some time for yourself during the next few days. Allow, at least, 30 minutes at a time and a couple of days in between each session.

2. Carry out a brain-storming activity where you write down your favourite areas of interest (i.e. music, health, economy, tourism). A feasibility assessment (i.e. "would I be able to earn enough working in this field?") is neither required, nor appropriate, at this stage.

3. Identify professional roles of interest within each of the areas above. For example, for music it could be a journalist specialising in jazz, disc jockey, band manager or event organiser; for health it could be a nurse or counsellor; for economy it could be an analyst or trader; for tourism it could be holiday representative, travel agent or guide.

4. Allow a 3-day break and, without looking at the above list of professional roles, write down a list of characteristics that you would value in your professional life (i.e. opportunity to develop personally, working environment, making a difference in people's life, financial reward, etc.).

5. Carry out an assessment of the importance of the above characteristics when compared to each other. For example, you may attribute a normal value to some (i.e. working environment and financial reward), and more value to others (i.e. personal development and making a difference in people's life). Once you have created your scale of values, give a weight to each value (i.e.

working environment = normal value = weight 1; personal development = double value = weight 2; making a difference in people's lives = triple value = weight 3).

6. Enter your roles and characteristics in your grid, as showed in Appendix C. Do not enter the weight of each characteristic in their cell, as you want to make sure that your initial scores are not affected by the concomitant appraisal of a characteristic's weight.

7. Make as many copies of the grid as the professional roles you have identified and, on different days, score just one role on each sheet by entering your values as Initial Scores (IS). This is done to ensure that you don't look at previous values as you score subsequent roles. I would recommend the use of a 1 to 10 scale for your scoring.

8. Transfer the Initial Scores (IS) and the weight of your characteristics on another sheet, as in Appendix D. Calculate the Weighted Values, write them down and then add them up. The results will show

you which roles would best match your desired characteristics.

9. Now, it's time to carry out a feasibility assessment. Starting from the role with the highest score, assess how feasible it is for you to train or re-train in the chosen roles. You may also wish to allow for a transitional period where you carry on your present occupation and train part-time for the new. You may then resign from the current job as soon as you feel ready to go for the new one. Some have also opted for working part-time in the old position, to make sure that enough money was coming in to pay for the bills, and began practising part-time the new activity. Some have actually found that they were already in the right job and carrying out this exercise provided them with a renewed motivation to continue and with a clearer insight into their personal issues (i.e. difficult relationships or unhealthy habits).

I have gone through the above process with a number of clients over the past ten years. In the end, they were surprised at how such a simple step-by-step activity enabled them to turn bleak scenarios, where apparently no way out could be found, into workable and stimulating alternatives.

Activities Box 11.

Time for your *PAL …*
*Think about the pace of life just 150 years ago. Then think about its speed now. What similarities and differences do you find?*

and for your *BIT.*
*Practise the 4-step personal orientation activity indicated on page 146 and/or the professional orientation one.*

# Chapter 6
# Relationships

*"Friendship is the most precious amongst all the good things we receive from wisdom. Each morning Friendship goes around the world to awaken humankind, so that we can greet one another joyfully."*
*Epicurus*

## Twelfth Step
## The interpersonal level

When we experience personal distress we are likely to withdraw from social contacts. Rationally we know that this is not appropriate and that isolating ourselves from the world does not do us any favour, but when you are there in the middle of the emotional storm picking up radio signals from the control room becomes very difficult.

Taking some time off to reflect on past events, current choices and future goals, is absolutely fine. There is a value in sadness and it lies in the chance that it allows us to reassess our decisions and readjust our route in the light of difficult times and situations, thus providing us with the opportunity to add meaning to our life.

The art of balancing the primordial survival instinct of looking after ourselves with the equally primeval drive towards interacting satisfactorily with fellow human beings will be the topic of this step. You will learn here how to improve your interpersonal relationships and how to deal with difficult ones.

First, I would like you to be fully aware that people are not just what they are, as physical entities. To us, each person we meet also represents the metaphor for something or someone else. So, for example, when a fifty-three year old man leaves behind a long-term relationship to start a fling with a much younger woman, what the man sees in her is not just youth or, possibly, beauty, but his own lost youth and his own lost beauty, and in embracing this adventure he is trying to recapture them.

So, let's take a closer look at interpersonal interactions: what are their main ingredients?

We do know that they are about sharing, but what is it that we are sharing with someone else at a given moment of our life?

There are two fundamental components to each relationship, whether we are in the presence of a personal interaction (i.e. siblings, friends, girlfriends) or a professional one (i.e. school mates, work colleagues). These components are intimacy and togetherness.

**Intimacy** consists of the meaningful situations we share, like open dialogues and confidences, physical closeness, sexual intercourse and other significant experiences. Intimacy is about giving and receiving. It may have its ups and downs like the tidal waves. One day you give, another you receive. You just go with the flow and enjoy it.

**Togetherness** consists of the motivation and willingness to share our interests and life projects. Please note that we say "share" and not "unconditionally accept" or "abide by", because you can, for example, share somebody's interest in the arts without feeling obliged spending hours in art galleries every time you visit a new town, or you can share your colleague's enthusiasm for a new project without totally agreeing with him on how to develop it.

Togetherness is about team work and being in the same boat rowing in the same direction. Togetherness is about mutual support.

Healthy relationships are the ones where there are elements of both components. When relationships are made only of elements of just one component, they are unbalanced and sooner or later problems will arise. Humans are not perfect and perfect relationships are not of this world. That's why it is so important to appreciate two main points:

a) Work is always in progress: if you want to make the most of an interpersonal interaction, be prepared to work on it, nicely, gently and, above all, constantly.

b) It takes two to tango: one thing is having ups and downs, as part of the normal games of intimacy, another is having a major unbalance at the togetherness level.

So, how do we work practically on improving our interpersonal skills?

### *Lesson 1. Relating is an art.*

Relating at the interpersonal level is an art, like relating at the intrapersonal and personal ones, not an exact science. Relating is the art of integrating intimacy and togetherness. You learn through experience and you experience through learning. So, to make sure that you are able to practise this art proficiently and satisfactorily you want to learn how to create a balance.

### *Lesson 2. Creating an internal balance.*

Healthy relationships comprise two balanced persons. If one isn't, the interpersonal interaction will not work. So, first of all, make sure that you are aware of where you are, at a given moment in time. Are you happy with your physical condition? Are you at peace with yourself? Do you think you are connected with your rational resources? If the answers to the above questions are not completely affirmative, do your own work first.

I once saw a pleasant lady who came to me because of difficulties in the relationship with her new partner. She felt very close to him, there were many things she liked about him and she was sure that he felt the same about her, but they seemed to have problems in communicating with each other, which would often result in unnecessary arguing and this started exacting its toll by making their interactions increasingly difficult.

She was genuinely puzzled when I suggested to work first on her own internal balance, as she was expecting me to address interpersonal issues straightaway. However, she took my word for it. After four meetings and before we even got started on their communication styles, she told me that her partner's behaviour had changed so significantly and their relating improved so much that it was not necessary to get into the second stage of our programme.

How come? Simply put, people respond to how we are, even before they process how we relate to them. Working on her internal balance made her realise that psychologically she was not in a comfortable place and that this uneasiness was filtering through to her partner who misinterpreted it as a sign that there was something wrong with him and their relationship, whereas her issues were of a different – and internal – nature.

By improving her internal balance she started sending out different signals (i.e. more relaxed and peaceful behaviours) to her partner, who, responded accordingly.

They say you cannot change the world. Well, I don't know about that. All I know is that when I am surrounded by nervous (or stressed, tired, etc.) persons this may affect me. Likewise I do feel different when in the company of relaxed (or happy, easy-going, etc.) people.

When we work on our internal balance, we become the persons we would like to be with, spreading healthy vibes all around and impacting in a helpful way on each person we meet.

If you feel balanced, you may wish to understand if your interlocutor is balanced too. If it is clear that they are not, see what you can do to help them. As we have just seen, being consistently balanced yourself can already help.

You don't want to impose your own person care model onto them (i.e. 'here, read this book and sort yourself out'), but you may ask how they are and if they know how to take care of their issues. Not knowing what to do or how to go about it is not a crime.

The point is, you don't want to waste your time with somebody who is not willing to look after themselves (because they don't want to or because they are not ready as yet).

***Lesson 3. Creating an interpersonal balance.***

An interpersonal balance is made up of five elements: both persons have the time and the space for being on their own, both persons have the time and the space for being with others, there is enough time and space for sharing intimacy and togetherness. If one of the above elements is missing, a relationship, of any nature, will not go very far.

If you notice a genuine interest in the person you are relating to in working on themselves and in improving your relationship there are a few things you can do:

- Make time to openly talk about your relationship.

- See if you can find a common ground to use as a safe base to leave from and come back to during your conversations.

- Be aware of your own behaviour and be ready to accept the other person's feedback on it (i.e. at times we are not aware of the tone of our voice, the expression of our face or the posture we assume, which can unwittingly become abusive or threatening).

- Agree on 'response delay' behaviours to adopt when one of the two doesn't feel ready to engage in a conversation about the relationship. So, for example, you may agree that it is ok to move to another room for a few minutes, or to colour code some behaviours and make the other aware of their colour at that moment in time ("oh dear, you are becoming deep purple ..."), or to write notes about what is bothering you which are then placed in a box, a pot or a drawer that the other can go and read when they feel ready.

As you can see, the above practical suggestions can be easily applied both in personal interactions (i.e. a sibling or a partner), and in professional ones (i.e. a work colleague or a fellow student).

***Lesson 4. Learning to let go.***

There is a time to work on a relationship and there is a time to let it go. Interpersonal interactions are supposed to be a 50-50 endeavour.

Sometimes the balance can go 60-40 or even 70-30 or 80-20, and that's fine provided that we go back to a point where both partners do their bit by rowing in the same direction.

However, many are stuck in co-dependent relationships, where they end up taking a lot of abuse and grief as a result of having become addicted either to another person, or to what this person represents to them (remember, people are also metaphors for something or someone else).

The point is: what is unhealthy for you cannot be healthy for someone else. I will clarify this with a real life example.

A young woman came to me complaining about her relationship with her partner. He was a heroine addict and had been feeding his addiction first with his own resources and then with hers. After years of empty promises of the kind "I will clean myself up as from tomorrow, next week or the beginning of the month", she had had enough but she felt unable to leave him when he seemed to need her most.

As you can see, she was playing the rescuer. For a number of reasons that it would not be appropriate to mention here, she had been performing the rescuer, the caring person who was always there ready to offer everything she had.

She did not realise how, in doing that, she was keeping her partner in a victim condition, thus reinforcing a situation that was deeply unhealthy for both.

When we take full responsibility for somebody's life, we take away from them the precious opportunity to learn how to take care of themselves.

When she finally decided to give him an ultimatum ("either you commit yourself to a rehabilitation programme or I'll leave and start a new life without you", he replied despondently ("go, I'll find somebody else").

So, she left and made a new start, which brought her a new job and a fulfilling relationship, and he was given back the choice to do what he wanted to do with his life.

A few weeks later he decided to clean himself up for good and about a year later he wrote a wonderful letter to her.

He thanked her for having made him realise how deep down he had got into his addiction and acknowledged how, by dissociating herself from this deeply hurtful experience, she gave him the chance to look and see how he was wasting his life. He was now back at work again and in a new relationship.

If you are currently stuck in a co-dependent relationship or you know somebody in such a situation, what you can do is to make the most of the few moments of clarity that you or your friend will still have and either go through this Artemíology programme from the beginning, or seek professional help.

Remember: if you partner is not willing to change, making a new start will benefit both of you. So, if you really care about somebody, sometimes letting go of them could be the most appropriate thing to do.

***Lesson 5. Getting out of the unhealthy triangle.***

As we have seen above, we may find ourselves trapped in an unhealthy and self-perpetuating victim-persecutor-rescuer spiral. When this happens, now you know what to do about it. To help you get straight to the point, I have provided an index of the exercises introduced in this guide in Appendix E.

To briefly sum up, if you feel you are in the 'victim' situation, practise the BBR, the Language Point and the SST. This will help you get out of the triangle, rather than moving to the 'persecutor' situation.

If you feel you are playing the 'persecutor', practise the BBR, the IB, the 3Bs, the PA and the SST. This will help you out of the triangle, rather than moving to the 'rescuer' situation.

If you feel you are acting as the 'rescuer', practise the BBR, the 3As and the SST. This will help you out of the triangle, rather than moving back to the 'victim' situation.

Naturally, the above suggestions are only meant as a shortcut to help you out in 'emergency' functioning. You are warmly encouraged to follow through the steps of this guide from the start, in the appropriate order.

Activities Box 12.

Time for your *PAL* …
*Think about one personal and one professional relationship you are currently engaged in. How balanced do you think they are, both internally and externally?*

and for your *BIT.*
*Practise the above lessons.*

# Chapter 7
# Behaviours

*"It is not our preferences that cause problems,
but our attachment to them."*

*Buddha*

## Thirteenth step
## Prevention is better than cure

This step will first explain what 'behavioural self-help' is about and why it works. You will then be introduced to three practical applications: the Magic Box, the Magic Purse and the Holy Place.

Please bear in mind that the following behavioural self-help techniques serve the purpose of providing an immediate support for when you are stuck in negative thinking or frequently experiencing the reoccurrence of unhealthy or self-harming behaviours (i.e. vomiting, self-cutting or withdrawing from social encounters).

You will be in a position to comprehensively address your issues – not only your behaviours – only once you will have gone through the learning process associated with the whole of the Artemíology programme.

The following letter was emailed to me by a girl in her early 20s, who wanted to get over her bulimia. I think it offers you a clear idea of what can go on in our mind, at times, and of why behavioural self-help interventions may be appropriate.

*"I have thought about your question 'What does bingeing do for me?' and came up with the following: It gives me something to do. This sounds terrible as it is such a waste of my health for such a silly reason, but it is part of the answer. If I am worried about something (usually work or my knee) and want to avoid these feelings, then this is the way I usually occupy myself and blot out the thoughts.*

*The same goes for being stressed/angry/upset. It helps to keep me in the same place. Part of me is scared of progressing at work or meeting new people by going out, or doing any other positive thing, and so I make myself sick as it keeps my self esteem in a low place. I can hide behind my eating disorder and not face up to the challenges of the real world.*

*As I have done it for many years now, it gives me security. I have binged many times without wanting to because I have been too scared to stay in the 'real world' and see what happens.*

*It also stops me from missing dancing. I am scared that if I go for long enough without being sick, I will become more in tune with my body and its need to dance. And then I will have to face up to the fact that my dream of a dancing career is never going to happen because my knee is such a mess. The more I am sick, the more numb I feel and the easier it is to cope with the fact that I can't dance."*

## *Help yourself!*

I have seen clients who were fully aware of their problems and knew fully well what to do. However, they asked for help in actually applying their knowledge to their everyday life. So, for example, I have worked with nutritionists and dieticians who knew what to eat and were dispensing sound advice every day to their clients, but then Dr Jekyll turned into

Mr Hyde and they would engage in bulimic or obsessive-compulsive behaviours. The same applies to other health professionals whom I have seen, who got themselves into drinking, drug abuse, smoking and gambling.

How is it that, even when we know that what we are doing is terribly wrong, we feel like we 'cannot' stop the urge to self-harm or dive into a spiral of negative thoughts?

There are two mind sets within each of us and these two 'persons' represent two very different sets of values: the inner adult and the inner child. Those of you familiar with Eric Berne's transactional analysis are advised that these two 'persons' are very different from Berne's ego states (i.e. the internal metaphors of parent, adult and child).

My view is that the inner adult is wise and takes time to consider things and situations. It is logical and able to deal with problems in an effective and rational way. Its downside is that, if left on its own, it can lead us into over-thinking and overworking.

The inner child, to the contrary, is the emotional and impulsive part of us. It is creative and has plenty of energy. However, it can get restless, is not interested in the future and by demanding immediate satisfaction NOW can become edgy and scream for attention.

When we try to be too good (i.e. perfectly sticking to a diet, impeccably going about our house work, precisely planning our day and week, etc.) the inner adult places too much pressure on the child, who sooner or later will either implode or explode.

Normally, nicer persons tend to implode, turning all this unhealthy energy onto themselves because they are sensitive and considerate individuals who will never hurt someone else, so they end up either experiencing high level of anxiety or harming themselves (i.e. bingeing and vomiting, starving, self-cutting, etc.).

Others explode, instead, and turn this energy against somebody else (i.e. hitting, swearing, threatening, plotting, etc.). The more pressure the adult puts on the child, the more powerful – and seemingly incontrollable and unstoppable – its reaction will be. That's why we feel like we 'cannot' stop the self-defeating behaviours, once we get started.

So, this is how it comes. Now, let's see how it goes.

If real children were sitting in a room playing with one of the many toys piled up beside them and you were to enter and place new toys close to them, what do you think their reaction would be? I tell you that a real child would go and play with the new toys, at least for a while, out of curiosity.

Does your inner child want to play an unhealthy game, yet again? Is it screaming for attention? Fine. Let's introduce new games for it to play. Let's hear what it wants to say. Let's channel this vast amount of energy into new equally exciting but less harmful activities.

***The Magic Box.***

The Magic Box will help you choose something else to do, rather than going straight for the self-harming behaviour or drifting into negative thinking. This self-help activity is designed for use at home. Before you use your Magic Box you want to create it. First, jot down a list of activities whose two main characteristics are:

1. they will keep you engaged for 5 to 15 minutes;
2. they are exciting, pleasurable or fun.

Thinking of your senses may help you with your list. For example, hearing can attract items like listening to your favourite song or singer, touch can attract items like rubbing your hands with a particular piece of cloth or hand-cream. Once the list is made, write the items, one by one, on separate little pieces of paper and fold them. Now buy or make a nice box (the nicer the better), one with a proper lid, and place your little pieces of paper in the box.

The next time you feel like your inner child is taking over, all you want to do is say to yourself "Ok. I am going to go for a big binge (or whatever your usual self-harming behaviour) in a moment, not just now" and, as you are saying this, you reach for the Magic Box, lift the lid, fish an item and carry out the activity indicated on the little piece of paper.

In 75-80% of cases, fishing once is enough for not wanting to go back to the original self-harming behaviour or for letting go of the negative thoughts. In the remaining cases, fishing twice does the trick. I have been passing on this technique for the past ten years and it has never happened so far that somebody has had to fish three times or that after the second fishing they went back and carried out the unhealthy behaviour.

Why does this simple technique work? We do know that self-harming urges are very powerful. At the same time, we also know that they are extremely transient: that is, once you manage to keep your mind off them for a little while by introducing a *response delay,* they pass and go, provided that you don't stage a fight *against* them.

If you fight, the inner child will win nine times out of ten and not because you are weak or hopeless or stupid, but because your inner child is in the here-and-now and the wise inner adult is in the future.

Another reason why the inner child will not respond to the rational adult is because when your urge comes about you get to a different place and the language spoken by your inner adult will be incomprehensible to the child in you. In these moments it is extremely difficult to think straight. I know this and that's why I am not asking you to think straight. What I would like you to do is to first acknowledge what is going on and calm down the child by saying: "Ok. I am listening to you. I am going to do as you wish, in a moment" and then give the child a new game to play.

In other words, you are trading an immediate behavioural response (i.e. going to the fridge) for another immediate behavioural response (i.e. going to the Magic Box). Even if you find it difficult to talk to the child and calm it down, go straightaway to the Magic Box, the alternative will still work because it will engage your inner child who will be very happy to fish and play new games.

***The Magic Purse.***

The Magic Purse is the outdoor version of the Magic Box. You may find it very useful when you are at work. You create the Magic Purse and use it exactly as you do with the Magic Box by unzipping the purse as you would lift the box's lid. The only difference is that the list of activities here are required to be compatible with your work environment. As self-harming behaviours at work tend to come about during the lunch break, you won't find it difficult to create a list of alternative activities to carry out.

Frequent items re-occurring on people's lists are: listening to their favourite music, exploring shop windows (and occasionally buying something, as a special treat), planning weekends or holidays.

***The Holy Place.***

Whether you are at home or at work, you can help yourself by introducing another *response delay* by choosing a place which, from that moment, becomes your Holy Place: that is, a place where, no matter what, you are going to go and spend two to three minutes each time your urge comes about.

Your Holy Place is an environment where you feel safe, comfortable and relaxed. It can be a chair, a sofa, a bed, a corridor, a flight of stairs or a room. Some of the people I have worked with have found it useful to go immediately to their chosen place (as an immediate behavioural response) when they felt the unhealthy urge coming, before doing anything else, because from that place it was then much easier to move on to the next helpful behaviour.

Activities Box 13.

Time for your *PAL* …
*Write down a list of the items to place in your Magic Box and Magic Purse. Think about what environment could become your Holy Place.*

and for your *BIT.*
*Practise the response delay techniques above.*

## Fourteenth step
## Riding the hungry tiger

When you are going through a difficult time, you may wish to remind yourself of the word 'Peckish' which is an acronym for:

**P**revention
**E**xercise
**C**hange
**K**eep in mind your new you
**I**gnore specific goals
**S**olving skills
**H**ave fun

The word ***Prevention*** is there to remind you that there is so much you can do to avoid getting yourself into difficult situations, which are likely to trigger unwanted behaviours. So, for example, if you are single and your issue is night bingeing and cravings for sugary stuff, why do you buy chocolate biscuits and keep them in your cupboard? I can hear you saying "I have bought them for my friends." Yes, right.

You see, the point is, there are no such things as little elves visiting your home at night and filling your cupboards and fridge with food. *You* have bought what is there in your house. So the next time you walk in a supermarket, make sure that you write *beforehand* a list of what you would like to buy, otherwise you will hear the little voices of many unhealthy foods calling your name (oh, yes, you know they call you by your first name). The reality is that each time you walk in a supermarket you are totally unaware of half of the things you end up buying and regularly forget half of the things that you wanted to buy before getting there.

How come? Are you so dumb? Of course, you are not! Truth is there are a lot of people working behind the scenes to make sure that when we enter a supermarket we buy a lot, and a lot of what *they* would like us to buy. These people know how to run their business.

The whole process that sees a product from its creation to its place on a shelf, from advertising to packaging, from deciding its name and size to its retail price, involve lots of fine minds, including psychologists too! That's why if you want to defend yourself from their tricks and traps, write your list at home and then, once in there, just follow your list and you will be fine.

Another practical example of *prevention is better than cure* is that of what to do during your daily breaks when you are a student. Many students I have worked with go directly to the kitchen and grab something to eat and this frequently triggers binges and subsequent vomiting or purging episodes. They are all bright individuals but when these moments come they all turn into Mr Hydes. In such cases it helps to write down, beforehand, a list of pleasurable and fun activities to carry out during breaks from study or work. So, when the time for a break comes, all you do is to have a look at the list and pick what you fancy at that time, rather than wandering like zombies towards the kitchen.

We have already talked about **Exercise**, so this is just a reminder to go for it, nicely and gently, and on a daily basis.

**Change** is there to remind you that if you are here, reading this book, it is because you are not entirely satisfied with your life, or, if you are a psychological practitioner, because you would like to learn about Artemíology. I normally find it useful, at this point, to present my own version of the Karpman's drama triangle. I do this to make you aware of the vicious spiral you may be stuck in and, hence, of the basic fact that change is desirable.

Draw a triangle upside down and write next to the top left angle the word 'rescuer', then write next to the top right angle the word 'persecutor', and, finally, write next to the lower angle the word 'victim'.

Some of us can get stuck in the following spiral: we start by taking care of people's responsibilities for them (rescuer) and then get angry with them for what we have done (persecutor), and, subsequently, feel used and sorry for ourselves (victim) and to feel better we start taking care of others' responsibilities again (back to rescuer). Naturally, we may start from any of the three above 'roles' and once in the spiral we find it difficult to get out.

In my experience, many start from feeling victims and then when they have had enough turn into persecutors, but they soon feel bad about it and start playing the rescuers until they become disillusioned and fall into a victim state again.

Whichever way you look at it, one thing is for sure: none of these three roles is healthy.

**Keep in mind your new you**, means that if you would like to become a more balanced and happy person it would help if you were able to visualise yourself as the person you would like to be some time in the near future.

In order to do that, you may practise a simple and effective technique, which I have called the **K-technique**. I would advise you to go through the following steps one at a time (i.e. one step a day).

First, sit comfortably, close your eyes and imagine yourself in the near future. You look happy and you are in a nice place, either on your own or with somebody. You are the person you would like to become. It doesn't matter if the picture is in black and white or in colour, or if it looks like a photo or it feels like a 3D image. What counts is that the image is clear and is right there at the centre of your inner screen.

Then, open up your eyes and write down an accurate description of your image (which from now on we will call, your 'K-image'). Now, read through your written account of the k-image, then close your eyes again and visualise it.

At this point you are ready for the final step, which is, you are now able to visualise your k-image with your eyes open. You may try, for example, to 'place it' on your desk or anywhere you like.

How do you use your K-image, once you have created it and practised its visualisation? What is its practical purpose? To illustrate how the K-image can help in real life situations I offer you the typical scenario of a professional woman who spends a good deal of her time at work between the meeting room (i.e. briefings, seminars, negotiations, etc.) and the staff room. Here in England meeting rooms are designed to abide by the following order of priority:

1. Tea and biscuits (necessary)
2. Furniture (basic to minimal)
3. People (optional to irrelevant)

So there you are in the middle of a boring presentation and the tray full of cheap biscuits is looking at you...it's having a laugh...it's calling your name...gosh, what are you going to do? Are you going to think that summer is coming and your skirt is getting despondently tighter? Are you going to remind yourself that if you pick just one biscuit, then a few others will follow?

For a while you will play the "yes" or "no" game. Shall I have one or shall I pass? Suddenly, almost by magic, the first biscuit materialises in your mouth, you are virtually unaware of how it got there. Then, a few others follow, and some more find their way from the tray to their new home. Next, you feel disgusted with yourself. How can you be so weak? And the self-blaming game begins.

You see, in the real life example above the unhealthy choice (biscuits, cigarettes, drinks, etc.) does not meet a proper challenge: it's a very strong *you* in the present (I am bored, stressed, tired, nervous) against a weak *you* in the future (if I eat this rubbish I will keep putting on weight, smoking and drinking will damage my health). Moreover, it is the inner child against the inner adult.

When you feel bored, stressed, tired or nervous, the inner adult is most likely to give way to the inner child. You want satisfaction NOW and go for the unhealthy choice.

The K-technique introduces what you are looking for: a real challenge to the naughty child, a proper contestant.

When you visualise the k-image next to the tray of biscuits, you can see you smiling and happy on one side and the tray of cheap biscuits on the other. That will remind you that this is your life and you do have a choice, whether to get one step closer to the new you, the happy person you would like to become (i.e. the slimmer, non-smoking, sober you), or to feed the unhappy person you are now and turn to the cheap biscuits (cigarettes or drinks), thus going back to the downward vicious spiral of self-blame, guilt, low self-esteem and more unhealthy behaviours.

Some blow up the k-image to a bigger size than the tempting unhealthy choice, to make it more powerful. Others may even talk and ask their k-image questions. Naturally the conversation goes on in their minds, if others are around.

If you are motivated or patient enough to create your k-image and practise its visualisation, you will reap your reward.

Why does the k-technique work? It works because when you visualise and connect with your k-image, you are accessing your inner wisdom, that is, someone or something (depending on the points of view) that will always guide you towards healthy, useful and helpful places.

I personally, visualise my k-image every morning on my kitchen table, when I am having breakfast. It helps me stay focussed on my next goal and when I get there I create a new image.

Visualising my k-image regularly also helps, because if and when I feel like using it, I am able to place it where I would like it to be quite easily.

**Ignore specific goals** simply means: it is ok to have plans, but if they are too detailed, you may end up setting the scene for a big disappointment if you fall short, even slightly, of your target.

**Solving skills** is there to remind you that there is so much you *can* do to get out of difficult situations, once you find yourself in one of them. It's never too late to start taking care of yourself. This guide provides you with plenty of tools to do that.

**Have fun** simply means that you can be very good at what you do, personally and professionally, while, at the same time, embracing a light-hearted approach to your everyday chores and affairs. The heaviness and seriousness so often associated with some of the roles we play in life, does nothing to improve the quantity or the quality of our performances, but it does take a toll on our health.

Activities Box 14.

| Time for your *PAL* …<br>*Reflect on the PECKISH system above: how many of the ideas introduced here are you already practising?*<br><br>and for your *BIT.*<br>*Create your K-image and practise the K-technique.* |
|---|

# Behaviours

## Fifteenth Step
## Relapse management

When do you know that you have left behind your troubles for good and you are never going to relapse again?

I have worked with clients that had been binge drinking (i.e. fifteen pints of beer in one night three times a week, or one bottle of wine every night for months) or chain-smoking (i.e. 60 cigarettes a day for years) or vomiting (i.e. making themselves sick not less than three times a day for years). In such cases, when do you think we can say that they have reached the safe land?

If the beer drinker would start drinking two pints a night twice a week and kept it like that for six months, would you consider them arrived? I would. If the wine drinker would begin drinking one glass of wine with their supper and kept it like that for five months, would you consider them arrived? I would.

If the chain-smoker would stop smoking, and kept it like that for a year, would you consider them arrived? I would. If the bulimic would stop vomiting and kept it like that for eight months, would you consider them arrived? I surely would.

So, what happens if the beer drinker partakes in a stag night, gets drunk and drinks ten pints of beer? What if the wine drinker celebrates their team victory in the premiership and drinks one bottle of wine in one night? What if the smoker goes to a conference and lights up a cigarette before and after their speech? What if the bulimic changes house and job in a matter of weeks and makes themselves sick twice in a week? Would I consider these persons back to square one again? Of course not.

Do not assume that successful recovery from your problem means that you will *never* go back, even for one single episode, to the behaviour, or feeling, or concern that brought you here in the first place.

We are humans. We are not computers. The simple fact that we may have an occasional relapse of an old unhealthy habit does not mean that we have gone back to be that old person again. We do know that relapses tend to decrease in frequency and severity with time, because we learn through experience how to prevent, defuse and manage potential triggers.

Even if some people take a bit longer to consolidate their new healthy habits, would you say that binge eating every six months is the same thing as doing it three times a week? Would you say that getting drunk every time your team wins a premiership title is the same thing as drinking every night? Would you say that smoking two cigarettes in a year is the same as smoking 60 a day? Would you say that vomiting twice a week every eight months is the same thing as doing it every day for years?

This will be like digging a hole in which sooner or later you will fall down and hurt yourself. I am not denying that some people may never go back. I am saying that we are humans, not computers that once programmed or re-programmed carry on like that forever. So the point is not whether we may relapse occasionally into an unhealthy behaviour. The point is what we do if and when we relapse.

If you were used to smoking 40 cigarettes a day and then you gradually decrease to 30, 20, 10 a day until you quit altogether, how do you deal with one cigarette smoked three months later?

If you see it as a failure, as a sign of weakness, you are in for big trouble. Because if you start the self-blaming game again, you get back into the downward vicious spiral, where the next steps are "I am worthless", "I am a lost cause", "What's the point?" and in no time you will be back to 40 cigarettes a day again.

If, however, you see it as a sign that you are a human being, and, as such, you are fallible and not perfect, you will be more likely to consider how you haven't smoked one cigarette for three months and that you are capable of waiting, at least, another three months for the next one, if the occasion will arise.

In the end, what counts is that you keep the motivation to look after yourself. You want to congratulate yourself on what you have managed to achieve and keep on looking forward.

Then again, I am not saying that we are all bound to go back, sooner or later, though episodically, to our issues. Some don't and that's great! Nevertheless, let's keep in mind that life is a process, where we experience given events and situations and learn from them.

So, let's stay focussed on the process and on our learning abilities, rather than on single episodes.

Most importantly, let's remind ourselves that each little thing we do every day to look after our physical, emotional or rational components, directly impacts on our wellbeing and contribute to our happiness.

Activities Box 15.

Time for your *PAL* …
*Reflect on the point introduced above: how would you know when you have become the person you would like to become?*

and for your *BIT*.
*Discuss the above with one of your friends.*

# Chapter 8
# Time Perspectives

*"No matter how difficult the past,*
*you can always make a new start today."*
*Buddha*

*"Two things must be cut short: the fear of the*
*future and the memory of past discomfort;*
*the former does not concern me yet, and*
*the latter does not concern me anymore."*
*Seneca*

Some people believe, either spontaneously or as a result of being brainwashed through years of psychoanalysis, that the past is past and you cannot change it.

Therefore, if you were unlucky with your parenting and early childhood experiences you are cursed for the rest of your life and will carry this heavy heap of rubbish with you wherever you go. The best you could hope for, to stay with this view, would be to gain a better understanding of the sort of garbage you are carrying around. This is supposed to help you bear the weight and ease the pain.

Stop this nonsense. Now! Free yourself from the paws of therapists who make a living out of helping you carry your weight around. Free yourself from the iron chains and leaden balls they have tied to your ankle.

Naturally, we are not able to jump in a time-machine, go back to our past and change it: this is not what I mean. My point is: our past and our experience of it changes as we grow and change. When we are stuck where we are, nothing changes, including our past. When we grow and learn and develop, our past changes with us, because the way we relate to it and experience it has also changed.

As kids our family table, the one where we used to have lunch and supper all together, might have looked huge, as adults it seems of a normal size, if not smallish. Why is that? The table is still the same. Yes, exactly! The table is still the same but two important things have changed: we have physically grown up and, as a result, we have now a different appreciation of its size and we have visited many more houses and places and we have seen much bigger tables.

No matter what has happened in our past, we are humans, we can change. We can, first, distance ourselves from it and, then, learn how to perceive it in a completely different light. Remember: we learn through experience and we experience through learning.

Life can bring us sorrow. Life can bring us understanding, peace of mind and joy. Life is not a persecutor or a rescuer. Life is life, that's all. The sooner we become aware of it the better.

So, stop moaning and blaming your current problems on your father, your mother, your siblings, your school or the weather of the place where you grew up (too cloudy or too sunny, too cold or too hot). Start taking responsibility for your life and make a new start. Now!

# Acknowledgements

The ideas which have inspired the creation of Artemíology originated back in 1991 as a result of my conversations with a dear friend, the Italian General Practitioner Dr Mauro Pesce.

My personal and professional development owes so much to my supervisor of many years, Dr Scott Borrelli. Sadly, Scott, as a physical person, is no longer with us, but he is very much alive, with his teachings, in most of what I do.

I am thankful to the many I have met and learnt from. In particular, my thoughts go to Lucia Cerciello Cingolani, Prof. Stephen Palmer, Deanne Jade, Jenny Sandelson, Lynne Kaye, Albert Ellis and Dr John Cobb.

Dr Robert Lefever has kindly granted me permission to utilise a section of his book (*Eating Disorders),* which I have included in Appendix B. I would like to acknowledge that with gratitude.

I would like to thank Steven Ardron for his valuable comments on the first edition of this guide.

Finally, a special "thank you" to Margaret Russo, who has helped turn the original manuscript of this work into the first edition.

# Appendix A

## *Frequently Asked Questions.*

*What do I think of diets?*

Diets are never the solution to your issues and are often the cause of your problems. Many develop serious illnesses and eating disorders as a result of a diet. So, what shall we do? You want to take care of your body by applying the advice and suggestions offered in this guide. There's no need to embark on yet another diet.

*What do I think of the Atkins diet?*

The Atkins diet is based upon four basic principles:

1. Limit and control certain carbohydrates to achieve and maintain a healthy weight.
2. Choose carbohydrates wisely (vegetables, fruits, legumes, whole grains), avoiding refined carbohydrates, hydrogenated oils and foods with added sugars.

3. Eat until you are satisfied and, to lose weight, focus on protein, leafy vegetables and healthy oils.
4. Everyone's metabolism and lifestyle are different. Discover your individual carbs level to achieve and maintain a healthy weight. (1)

The Atkins diet has the merit of having drawn people's attention to the fact that a healthy eating style is one which includes fats and does without, or sensibly reduces, refined carbohydrates and sugars, most of which are *hidden* in foods which we deem as healthy (i.e. sauces or cereals).

The downside is that people usually approach this diet in a very unbalanced way, that is, they immediately cut down on carbohydrates and exceed with protein consumption, rather than continuing having quality carbohydrates at their meals.

*How much carbohydrates should you eat?*

Carbs provide fuel. So how much your body requires depends on how you use it. Bear in mind that up to one third of the energy you produce is used by your brain alone, so whatever you do, make sure that you eat a good source of carbs at each meal.

*How much proteins should you eat?*

You have developed your muscle system and bones structure, thanks to the consumption of proteins. The functioning of the immune system requires proteins too. Naturally, adults still require proteins to keep their muscle tone and bone density and for the production of certain hormones – like the one regulating the functioning of the thyroid. A healthy male should eat between 50 and 55 grams of protein a day. A healthy female between 45 and 50. To give you a practical idea of what that means, consider that when you eat 100 grams of fish or meat you provide your body with approximately 25 grams of proteins.

*How much fat should you eat?*

State Registered Dieticians say: "*Fat is often given a bad name. We only need to watch the television advertisements or walk around the supermarket to be reminded that we should be reducing the level of fat in our diet. This is often taken to extremes. Fat is* ***essential*** *for life. It is recommended that between 30 and 35% of our* *energy intake* ***should*** *come from fat. There are three types of fat – saturated fats, polyunsaturated fats and monounsaturated fats.* ***We need all types of fat in our diet.*** *No fat is 'bad'.*

*Following a diet* ***too low in fat*** *is likely to:*

1. *Lead to a greater preoccupation with food. This could increase a person's risk of bingeing.*
2. *Make you feel hungry. Fat helps increase satiety levels. Including fat at mealtimes reduces the likelihood of snacking between meals.*
3. *Lead to nutritional deficiencies.*

*For females, approximately 20 to 25% of the body weight should be fat. For males it is approximately 10 to 15%. Levels lower than this are likely to lower resistance to disease, cause weakness, irritability and affect fertility.*

*Fat is* ***essential*** *to:*

- *Keep us warm.*
- *Protect our internal organs from impacts such as a fall.*
- *Provide us with essential fatty acids, which we need to eat on a* ***daily*** *basis. These are essential for brain function and*

*in the prevention of heart disease. Essential fatty acids are extremely important to the growing foetus for normal brain development.*

- *Contribute to the structure of blood vessels.*
- *Coat our skin with a thin but essential layer. Detergents remove this layer causing dry skin. The skin will secrete more fats which build up to normal levels after a few days.*
- *Transport cholesterol around the body. Cholesterol levels are often raised if you are avoiding fat. The exact explanation for this is unknown although if you reintroduce more fat into your diet following a period of restriction, your cholesterol level will fall.*
- *Contribute to the structure of hormones, for example oestrogen. For women, reduced oestrogen will have a knock on effect, i.e. lack of periods increasing the risk of osteoporosis.*
- *Provide us with fat soluble vitamins, i.e. vitamin A. This vitamin is required for growth and repair of tissues, i.e. muscles such as your heart". (2)*

*Which fats should you favour?*

As Meredith Small notes *"...the most dramatic change in what we eat has happened in the past century, with industrialisation and the development of the food industry. Manufacturers favour foods with long shelf lives, so they mostly use soy, corn, palm and cottonseed oil. All contain high amounts of omega-6 fatty acids and very little omega-3, a balance that is further skewed when the oils are hydrogenated to make them keep even longer. According to Hibbeln, the average annual consumption of soy oil in the US stands at 11 kilograms, a thousand fold increase in less than 100 years. It accounts for 83 per cent of all the fats we eat. And while we ladle on the omega-6s, most of us eat few of the foods that are high in omega-3s such as oily fish, walnuts, flax seed and olive oil. As a result, our diets now contain 16 times as much omega-6 as omega-3, whereas a century ago we would have been getting about equal amounts of each. 'Nobody could adjust that fast', says Hibbeln".* (3)

*Is snacking a healthy or an unhealthy habit?*

As Dr Lefever observes: *"Chewing stimulates the appetite centre of the brain. Once stimulated, it remains 'turned on' for about twenty minutes. Grazing between meals can therefore result in a constant feeling of hunger or expectation of food. For the same reason it is possible still to feel hungry after a vast, but rapid, binge."* (4)

*Is irregular eating predisposing you to weight gain?*

According to the International Journal of Obesity, irregular eating decreases the thermic effect of food compared to regular eating even in thin people, thus the answer is affirmative: irregular eating will predispose to obesity.

*How often should you weigh yourselves?*

As far as I am concerned, you may as well throw your scale in the bin: scales always tell lies. What is the meaning of a scale value? Does it say anything about how much muscle, bones and fat cells your body is made of? You may be losing weight and be happy by adhering to a very unhealthy diet which is making you lose precious muscle and bone density rather than fat cells. You may be gaining weight thanks to a balanced diet which is making you lose all the unwanted fat zones but is strengthening your muscles and bones. Which option would you choose? Would you rather weigh 55 Kg and be rundown and flabby, or weigh 60 Kg and be fit and slim?

People going on a diet are not concerned about numbers! They fret about their shape. They mourn about the loss of not being able to fit in a pair of jeans that they have been able to wear for the past seven years. Now, whether it is realistic to expect that a 30 year old woman may still fit in the same size of trousers she would wear when 18, that's another issue. The point I am making here is that your scale says nothing about your fitness and shape: it gives you just a meaningless number. Muscle and bones cells are comparatively heavier than fat cells: your scale says nothing about that!

So, what I suggest you to do is to find your 'shape indicator' to help you monitor on a monthly basis how you take care of your body. Choose an item from your wardrobe (i.e. a pair of trousers, a dress, etc.) and try it on to check your overall shape and which parts of your body you will like to work on. This way, rather than fretting about a meaningless number, you will be able to focus your energy on specific areas of your body you would like to work on through general or targeted forms of exercise and balanced eating.

*How do you know if you are not eating enough?*

You will experience any, or a combination, of the following symptoms:

"Emotional
1. Depression
2. Irritability and anxiety
3. Muddled natural instincts
4. Progressive withdrawal and isolation

Behavioural
1. Dramatic increase in preoccupation with food
2. Total devotion to feeding others
3. Eating slowly and chewing thoroughly
4. Increased hunger (intolerable)

Physical

1. Gastro-intestinal discomfort
2. Decreased need for sleep
3. Dizziness, headaches
4. Hypersensitivity to noise and light
5. Reduced strength
6. Hair loss
7. Poor tolerance of cold temperatures" (5)

*Are you sugar sensitive?*

If you have been brought up eating lots of sugary stuff, chances are that you are. Sugar sensitivity has been linked with alcohol addiction and binge eating. To find out more about this I would warmly recommend the reading of *Potatoes not Prozac*, by Kathleen Des Maisons. The full reference is indicated in the Resources section of this guide.

*Are you drinking enough water?*

75% of Americans are chronically dehydrated (this finding may apply to half the world's population). In 37% of Americans, the thirst mechanism is so weak that it is often mistaken for hunger. Even mild dehydration will slow down one's metabolism as much as 3%. One glass of water shuts down midnight hunger pangs for almost 100% of the dieters studied in a University of Washington study. Lack of water is the number 1 trigger of daytime fatigue.

Preliminary research indicates that 8-10 glasses of water a day could significantly ease back and joint pain for up to 80% of sufferers. A mere 2% drop in body water can trigger fuzzy short-term memory, trouble with basic math and difficulty focusing on the computer screen or on a printed page. Drinking 5 glasses of water daily decreases the risk of colon cancer by 45%, plus it can slash the risk of breast cancer by 79%, and one is 50% less likely to develop bladder cancer. (6)

## Appendix B

### *General Information About Eating*

( reproduced with permission from Dr Robert Lefever's book '*Eating Disorder'* )

Eating should be a pleasure: the taste and process of eating should be enjoyable.

Fluid retention, diabetes, thyroid deficiency and various other medical conditions can have an effect on body weight but can easily be controlled medically and should have no effect on the simultaneous treatment of an eating disorder.

As a general rule for good health one should drink one and a half to two litres (seven to ten cups) of fluid each day.

Bottled sauces are best avoided because many of them contain sugar or white flour or they may be very spicy and stimulate the appetite. They may also blunt the palate so that it becomes progressively less sensitive to delicate flavouring.

Appetite suppressants should be totally avoided because they are addictive. It should be realised that nicotine, caffeine and diet drinks tend to be used as appetite suppressants and these substances are in any case addictive in their own right, whatever the reason for their use.

Laxatives should be avoided because they form part of the binge/purge behavioural addiction component of an eating disorder. Bowel function takes time to return to normal after years of abuse through an eating disorder. Patients with anorexia, for example, will often complain that they are "constipated" when what they mean is that they have the sensation of something in their bowels. This sensation is therefore not due to constipation but to hypersensitivity as a result of years of starvation.

Taking regular exercise is healthy but as little as twenty or thirty minutes a day for three days a week is quite healthy enough. Exercise and the "high" it can produce can become an addiction in itself.

It takes about ten days for the emotional high and subsequent withdrawal symptoms from sugar to clear. Each sugar binge will result in its own withdrawal period.

If you experience any cravings to binge, purge or starve you should share these feelings with someone at the time, if this is possible. Cravings are not something to be ashamed about. Nor are they a sign that things are going badly. Indeed, they are entirely normal and they are common for an addict in early recovery.

So-called “forbidden foods”, particularly in anorexic patients, tend to become an obsession. These patients often make lists of forbidden foods – usually fats, meats and carbohydrates – that are all perfectly healthy. This obsession can even sometimes take the form of supposed food allergies and tactical vegetarianism (designed to produce weight loss, rather than from philosophical conviction). When we come into recovery it is important to reconsider what we are prepared to eat.

Meal times should be as regular as possible. Some sufferers find excuses to have breakfast at 5am or put dinner off until 11pm. We need to learn to keep within normal parameters, such as having breakfast at 7 - 9am, lunch at 12 - 2pm and dinner at 7 - 9pm. These are guidelines only and may not suit shift work. However, it is important to have three meals well spaced throughout the working hours.

Some guidance may be useful on the concept of normal eating, but making out particular “food plans” or having “food sponsors” can be dangerously obsessive. It gives food a power that it does not possess. There is no need to count out exact weights, portions or calories. We need to learn to eat according to genuine physical hunger rather than emotional cravings.

# Appendix C

## *Professional Orientation Grid (Blank)*

| | Journalist | Counsellor | Trader | Travel Agent |
|---|---|---|---|---|
| Working environment | | | | |
| Financial reward | | | | |
| Personal development | | | | |
| Making a difference in people's life | | | | |

# Appendix D

## *Professional Orientation Grid (Completed)*

| | Journalist | | Counsellor | | Trader | | Travel Agent | |
|---|---|---|---|---|---|---|---|---|
| | IS | WV | IS | WV | IS | WV | IS | WV |
| Working environment Weight 1 | 5 | 5 | 6 | 6 | 7 | 7 | 6 | 6 |
| Financial reward Weight 1 | 6 | 6 | 5 | 5 | 9 | 9 | 6 | 6 |
| Personal development Weight 2 | 6 | 12 | 8 | 16 | 5 | 10 | 6 | 12 |
| Making a difference In people's life Weight 3 | 6 | 18 | 8 | 24 | 4 | 12 | 5 | 15 |
| | | 41 | | 51 | | 38 | | 39 |

# Appendix E

## Index of Exercises

# Notes

## Chapter 1.

1. Online Thesaurus, 2014: *www.**thesaurus**.com/browse/**happiness***

## Appendix A – Frequently Asked Questions

1. 'Introducing the Atkins food pyramid' leaflet (2004).
2. Hand-out produced by State Registered Dieticians at Portsmouth Hospitals NHS Trust.
3. Small (2002).
4. Lefever (2003).
5. Hand-out produced by State Registered Dieticians at Portsmouth Hospitals NHS Trust.
6. Hand-out released by the National Centre for Eating Disorders (UK).

# Bibliography

## *Books*

Assagioli, R. (1971) *Psychosynthesis*, New York: Viking.

Beck, A. T. (1991) *Cognitive Therapy and the Emotional Disorders*, London: Penguin Books.

Bellino, F. (1988) *Etica della Solidarieta` e Societa` Complessa (Ethics of Solidarity and Complex Society)*, Bari: Levante.

Bettelheim, B. (1982) *Freud and Man's Soul*, London: Penguin Books.

Borrelli, S. E. & Palumbo, T. (2004) *Italy,* in Malley-Morrison K. (ed.) *International Perspectives on Family Violence and Abuse*, Mahwah (NJ): Lawrence Erlbaum Associates.

De Crescenzo, L. (1983) *Storia della Filosofia Greca – I Presocratici (History of Greek Philosophy, Part 1)*, Milano: Mondadori.

De Crescenzo, L. (1986) *Storia della Filosofia Greca – Da Socrate in poi (History of Greek Philosophy, Part 2)*, Milano: Mondadori.

De Crescenzo, L. (2002) *Storia della Filosofia Medioevale (History of Medieval Philosophy)*, Milano: Mondadori

Dryden, W. (1999) *Rational Emotive Behavioural Counselling in Action*, London: Sage.

Filippani-Ronconi, P. (1994) *Il Buddismo (Buddhism)*, Roma: Newton Compton.

Freud, A. (1993) *Anna Freud: Her Life and Work*, London: Freud Museum Publications.

Freud, S. (1991) *Introductory Lectures on Psychoanalysis*, London: Penguin Books.

Furedi, F. (2004) *Therapy Culture*, London: Routledge.

Goleman, D. (1995) *Emotional Intelligence*, Glasgow: ThorsonsAudio.

Gross, R. D. (1999) Psychology: *The Science of Mind and Behaviour*, London: Hodder & Stoughton.

Hadot, P. (1999) *Philosophy as a Way of Life*, Oxford: Blackwell.

Hirst, B. (2002) *Il riso non cresce sugli alberi (Rice does not grow on trees)*, Milano: La Tartaruga.

Jacobs, M. (2002) *Psychodynamic Counselling in Action*, London: Sage.

Kornfield, J. (1994) *Buddha's Little Instruction Book*, New York: Bantam Books.

Laszlo, E. (1978) in Bellino, F. (1988) *Etica della Solidarieta` e Societa` Complessa (Ethics of Solidarity and Complex Society)*, Bari: Levante.

Lazarus, A. A. (1997) *Brief but Comprehensive Psychotherapy*, New York: Springer.

Lawrence, J. in *The Bathroom Inspiration Book*, Saddle River (NJ): Red-Letter Press.

Lefever, R. (2003) *Eating Disorders*, Nonington (Kent): Promis.

Lerner, M. D. and Sheldon, R. D. *Acute Traumatic Stress Management*, New York: AAETS.

Petronio, G. (1977) *Italia Letteraria (History of Italian Literature)*, Roma: Palumbo.

Pinel, J. P. J. (2003) *Biopsychology*, Boston: Allyn and Bacon.

Smail, D. (1993) *The Origins of Unhappiness*, London: Harper Collins.

Smail, D. (1998) *How To Survive Without Psychotherapy*, London: Constable.

Thich Nhat Hanh (1997) in Luchinger, T. *Steps of Mindfulness (video)*, Zurich: Luchinger.

Vinay, M.P. (1973) *Hygiene Mentale (Mental Hygiene)*, St Francois Sherbrooke: Editions Paulines.

## *Articles and papers*


Burne, J. (2004) *Can this man cure your depression?* The Independent Review, 17 May 2004.

Canter, D. (2002) *The rise and rise of biobabble*, New Scientist, Vol. 173, issue 2336, 30 March 2002, p. 50.

Davidson, R. (2004) in Huppert, Baylis, Keverne (2004) *The science of well-being*, The Psychologist, Vol. 17, No. 1, p. 7.

Deary, I. (2003) *Ten Things I hate about Intelligence Research*,
The Psychologist, Vol. 16, No 10, p. 537.

Fairburn, C. G. and Harrison P. J. (2003) *Eating Disorders*, Lancet 2003; 361: 407-16.

Farley, P. (2004) *The anatomy of despair*, New Scientist, Vol. 182, issue 2445, 01 May 2004, p. 42.

Healy (1998) in Palumbo, T. (1999) *A brief Introduction to Essential Psychology*, London (unpublished paper).

Lanza del Vasto (1975), poet, Christian mystic and non-violent activist, Fellowship Magazine, Sept. 1975.

Lawson, W. (2004) *The Glee Club*, Psychology Today, February 2004, p. 34.

Malley-Morrison, K. (2004) *The Evil of Inaction*, Talk given to graduating MA students, Boston University, 16 May 2004.

Palumbo, T. (1999) *A brief Introduction to Essential Psychology*, CMQ, Vol. X, No. 2 (286), London: GCD.

Pointon, C. (2004) *The future of trauma work*, Counselling and Psychotherapy Journal UK, May 2004, p. 10.

Rowe, D. (2001) *The story of depression*, Counselling and Psychotherapy Journal UK, November 2001, p. 5.

Small, M. F. (2002) *The happy fat*, New Scientist, Vol. 175, issue 2357, 24 August 2002, p. 34.

Thernstrom, M. (2001) *Life Without Pain*, The New York Times Magazine, December 16, 2001, New York.

Van der Kolk, B. A. (2002) *EMDR, Consciousness and the body*, Boston: The Trauma Center.

# Resources

## How to contact the Author

To contact Tommaso Palumbo please write to:
tom@tommasopalumbo.com

## Books

DesMaisons, K. (2001) *Potatoes not Prozac*, London: Simon & Schuster.

Masson, J. (1997) *Against Therapy*, London: HarperCollins.

Kornfield, J. (1994) *Buddha's Little Instruction Book*, New York: Bantam Books.

De Botton, A. (2001) *The Consolations of Philosophy,* Penguin: London.

Palumbo, T. (2017) *Handbook of Active Meditation ~ Peaceflow in Action,* London.